VOLUME 1

The Unconventional CEO·

COMMON SENSE BEYOND CONVENTIONAL MANAGEMENT THINKING

MARIO PRETORIUS

Second Edition, 2020

ISBN: 978-1-77605-666-8

Produced by Kwarts Publishers
www.kwartspublishers.co.za

Contact the author:
Mario Pretorius
www.mariopretorius.co.za
Mobile: +27 836412000
mp@valcapital.co.za

Do what's right
and
fear no-one

Contents

What They Are Saying About *The Unconventional CEO*

I have benefited from having known Mario Pretorius since Student Council days, which should have prepared me for his unconventional approach to life and business. I have to admit that I am impressed with his passionate and analytical dissection of a wide range of topical management issues in *The Unconventional CEO*. Business leaders may believe that they understand the importance of people, cash flow and ethics (or should I say honesty?) but prepare yourself to be enlightened by Mario's straight-shooting. Read it at your peril, because you will need stamina and concentration to absorb a lifetime of wisdom which has been crystallised into a number of well-written one-pagers.

You will find no attempt in the book to tell you **how** to run your business, but rather a number of very well thought out pointers on **what** to manage. Don't be mistaken; true to himself, Mario encourages you to focus on the **how** rather on the **what**. It is difficult to decide what impressed me most. Mario's analytical ability or his unwavering emphasis of a CEO's need to be his people's champion? A must read!

Fritz Eloff
CEO
Kibernetika (Pty) Limited, Pretoria

As Chief Learning Officer of Naspers I am inundated with presentations on Leadership Programmes. To put it mildly, I am more often than not disappointed, because the offerings cater to management fads: knee-jerking to clichés and avoiding the hard issues. In short, the content focuses on creating cheerleaders instead of leaders. No wonder Peter Drucker once asked the rhetorical question: "Why are there so many management gurus? It's because the word charlatan is too difficult to spell."

Mario Pretorius' book avoids the clichés, does not cater to fashion or fad, and (his wisdom) comes from the trenches. There is no odour of academia, yet it is carefully considered, and is the product of an inveterate reader. I wish that we had more of this! I wish that I had all this information at my disposal twenty years ago when I started out on my consulting career – that lowliest of business models to which Mario refers: selling expertise. But then, not all of us have the full portfolio of capabilities to create the level of entrepreneurial business success Mario has managed to achieve.

Bertie du Plessis
Chief Learning Officer
Naspers Ltd, Amsterdam

This book, written by a serial entrepreneur who heads up a successful start-up that outperforms its peers, tells not only how to build a successful business, but also how to make it a lasting success. Young entrepreneurs and seasoned managers alike will derive great value from it, as will those who have been around the block a bit and who may have fallen into a comfortable routine of complacency. Those who may think life has become a bit of a slam dunk and who run the risk of being outsmarted, or outperformed, by someone who is just a little more focused or a little less afraid of failure. Those who are in need of a wake-up call.

Mario's book on enterprise management is just such a manual. If anything remotely similar was written for lawyers it would tell you when to sit, when to stand, when to talk and when to shut up, how to successfully plead guilty (and not get fired by your non-paying customer), what to do to make sure you are rewarded for your efforts, how to get paying customers, how to keep them and, very importantly, how to impress them enough to get them to actually pay you for your work.

It's a very good read.

Niël Pretorius
CEO
DRD Gold Ltd, Johannesburg

Reading Mario's book, I am reminded of the quote from Shakespeare's 'Julius Caesar, where Brutus records:

> *"There is a tide in the affairs of men.*
> *Which, taken at the flood, leads on to fortune;*
> *Omitted, all the voyage of their life*
> *Is bound in shallows and in miseries.*
> *On such a full sea are we now afloat,*
> *And we must take the current when it serves,*
> *Or lose our ventures."*

Mario is the philosopher captain, on a full sea, taking his fleet of ships through the currents and playing the game of business wisely for his ventures. He brings together a coherent picture of leading a business encompassing both 'hard' and 'soft' elements. Business schools tend to focus on the 'hard' elements, but in his book Mario points out how important it is to inspire and develop his loyal workforce, peopled by individuals who want to be part of the success, who bring their strengths to the business and are allowed to play to them.

So many companies fail to engage their people – some 20% in first-world countries are actively disengaged and damaging their employers' businesses. The philosophy outlined in this book goes a long way to identifying the fundamentals – hard as they are to implement well.

Ian Thomson
CEO
Leadership International PLC, Glasgow

Mario Pretorius' Biography

So far my luck is holding out. I have spent a lifetime preparing for things that may never happen; the peaceful revolutions and the earth-shattering theories. On the way, I picked up an MBA from the Graduate School of Business (GSB) in Cape Town and attended some postgraduate courses at the GSB, as well as Harvard Business School. My working experience includes multiple-year stints in Oslo, Milwaukee, Toledo and Ann Arbor, Michigan.

My corporate life included the very large (South African Breweries), the large (Malbak Subsidiaries) and the medium. I have listed three companies on the Johannesburg Stock Exchange (JSE Ltd). Because, but mostly in spite of, my best efforts, I have succeeded in business in multiple disciplines as founder and owner, across various industries, from property development to telecommunications. Through the Junior Chamber of Commerce I visited many countries, made lifelong friends and acquired an appetite for learning and understanding. Currently, I serve as CEO of TeleMasters Holding Ltd and on the boards of a number of companies and organisations.

My full bio is on LinkedIn and on Who's Who. You can follow me on Twitter here: @unconCEO. My website is www.MarioPretorius.co.za. Please feel free to contact me.

DEDICATION

To those masters whose magic rubbed off on me, although it took a long, long time to sink into my DNA. Thank you Fred, Svein, Phil, Ron, Meyer, Ian, Natie, Elmarie, Leon, Stephen and Terry for the good stuff.

Without a proper set of enemies I would have taken longer to pay the school fees. Wry appreciation to Aida, Austin, Chris, James and Tito.

The best lessons are learnt, practised and refined in family life. I have had ample opportunities on both sides of family management, the receiving and the dishing out.

My late dad, Willem, taught me resilience, often in a hard way that imprinted the lesson on the lazy student.

My mother, Joan, embodies a life dedicated to constant learning. While choosing the unconventional path less travelled, she still made life decisions with long-time horizons. This served as a template for my life.

My wife, Leanette, and daughters tolerate and support my time-consuming dedication to add meaning and livelihood to the people that chose to work in my enterprises. I have become who I wanted to be because of all your inspiration, guidance, encouragement and care. Thank you for every precious lesson.

DEAR CEO

It is more effective to have A Way of Doing Things than to have A Goal.

Asked what his ultimate goal was, world-famous golfer Nick Price said: "Goal? To play perfect golf. If I do that, winning will follow".

Goals are transient, changeable and there's nothing left to do after the goal has been achieved. That great Russian General Gregory Potemkin, having risen from being a peasant's son to achieving the greatest power in Russia, lamented: "Everything I have ever wanted, I have. I am entirely happy". He then locked himself away, alone. Potemkin suffered bitterly from having nothing left to want.

In striving for a way to do things, the actions you implement become a habit and therefore enforce permanent change. Each goal you have reached comes and goes as a waypoint on your ascent.

Your personal philosophy will determine your business style. After all, you are you and your management style is an extension of your thinking and skills. You are expected to be a Philosopher King, in the Platonic tradition. There are policies and procedures in place but they will be implemented in your style – what's most important, what's superfluous, what will please you. Take a bit of time to evaluate their effect on your enterprise's success.

You came to hold your position on the strengths of **what** you achieved, **how** you achieved it, as well as **how** you will get everybody on your side to achieve what is expected by you from them all. Good luck. The lifespan at the top is mercilessly short, often mercifully so.

While you are standing at the pinnacle, surveying the battlefield before you and reviewing your troops, here are some truisms that might clarify some of your own thoughts, provoke a new understanding, or add an insight.

I have written down what I learned from the School of Hard Knocks, from contemporaries and from other sages, and not from the literature on business and management. It should form a little addendum, and even an antidote, to the conventional and often fast-changing management whims being taught at the Business schools where I had my own fair share of indoctrination, and my doubts over the wisdom being dispensed.

Maybe your aim, too, is to do perfect business. That has become my way.

Please share your experiences, your wise insights and your how-not-to's. There is a world of neophytes out there who want to know the reality and what works, as opposed to the ivory tower missives rained onto them by those with tenure.

Maybe we can share from experience and together we can learn more easily. It's worth a good try.

Mario Pretorius
Pretoria, October 2014

1.

THE BUSINESS TEST FOR SOUND STRATEGY IS THE ANSWER TO THE QUESTION: HOW?

Many temptations are disguised as wonderful opportunities. The do-ability, the feasibility and the good-for-us factor are determined by the **how**. Do we have the expertise? If not, **how** will we acquire it? If we can get it, **how** will we generate the cash to pay for it? The list is endless, but the biggest **how's** must be answered in a persuasive, cogent way. There is no movement if the organisation is not capable of executing strategy; all other actions are self-deceiving wish lists and dreams of higher pay rungs.

The business model hinges on the **how**. Often the best strategy is just improving the **how** incrementally, moving ever so slowly forward to nose in front of a competitor, whose never-ending jamborees and strategy sessions generate more questions than answers. Your **how** *is* your business, so any change in **how** must be carefully weighed. There are many unintended consequences – usually more detrimental than what Santa Claus brings.

I once witnessed an entire strategy presentation being demolished in two words. It was a 1989 Protea Data annual board presentation about capturing a 5% market share for a new printer line. Chairman Hugh Brown simply asked of the 5% target: "**Why?**"

The Sales Director answer: "Because without getting to 5% we would not have a feasible business and we're sure to get there."

The chairman then asked: "**How?**"

The demotion of the hapless chap came swiftly afterwards. Dreams are not strategy; they are visions and illusions of the future, unless the crucial question **how** is answered.

2.

THERE IS A WORLD OF DIFFERENCE BETWEEN KNOWING WHAT AND KNOWING HOW

Many strategies are thick and fast on the **what**. The thinking is clear, the actions are cogent, the strategy is as sensible in terms of morality as it is in intended benefit. A quick march to Moscow before the snow sets in. Destruction of the Soviet bases behind the Urals. *Voilà!* The oil riches secured would have fuelled the *Wehrmacht* and *lebensraum* would have extended to the Pacific. Yes, these strategies make perfect sense, with reasons to go to war.

There is no disputing the **what**. There are a dozen codicils on expanding the **what,** with good cheer and with supreme acceptance, a round of applause, please?

The confusion with the **how** often concerns its extrapolation. We must continue as before; only more so. Shall we stick to what we know? Then the prize will surely be ours? No! Playing safe will not get you to the stars.

It reeks that so many ventures end up on the rocks of hard reality because no-one included the **how** and no-one else impertinently and insistently asked about the **how's**.

The reserves must be fresh. There must be ample time to revisit the inconveniences when reality sets in and the enemy countermoves. There must be the will to innovate and compromise and somehow produce the **how** in dire circumstances. There are no medals for those who perish in sight of the finish line. It must be crossed, the **what,** and this will be achieved by the **how**.

3.

SELL YOUR PRODUCT IN THE WAY YOU WOULD WANT TO BUY IT

This is probably Rule #1 for success and yet such rules are so often more honoured in the breach than in the observance. Is it not imperative that you should consider your offering through the eyes of the user?

We use this determining test of going to market: how would we want to be approached, and what would make us buy it?

- With a one-page contract, in plain English? Check.
- With a guarantee that it will work in the way intended, perpetually. Or we will offer immediate cancellation of the contract if it doesn't? Check.
- There will be free support, on-site, 24/7. With no excuses or questions asked? Check.
- A single call to us will reach a person with a solution? Check.
- There will be monthly, quantified, feedback on whether the advantage which had been promised has materialised? Check.
- There will be an ongoing relationship with a pleasant and supportive human being? Check.
- We will present frequent options for improvement to what we offer, as the market changes, without obligation? Check.

The list goes on, with easy-to-understand, visible benefits and more. Check and check again. Check your offering often and make it an easy and compelling choice for your customers.

The best test for sustainable, ethical, no-nonsense business is to structure the offering, in economic, supportive and trust-wise terms, in the way that *you* would want to buy it. This pits your own thoughts of what is desirable against what your competition offers. This will loosen the juices of innovation and simplicity. Why in the world would you *not* want to buy this? In full trust, in mere seconds, with just a handshake, in the firm belief that all risks have been curtailed and all benefits will flow immediately? Is that what your people are offering? Pitching this no-brainer, presenting the best product, and with the service to back it up?

It may be costly. It may be very difficult to offer and sustain your **how** of a no-risk, instant-trust hand-shaker and ground breaker, but that's what it takes. Everyone wants the head honcho to sign-off with the customer, to give that final welcome-aboard stamp of approval. Get your people to think like this, too. **How** would they want to be convinced to say "yes!" to their own offering, and then **how** should they adapt it so it meets this requirement?

The mindset of the organisation is determined by the confidence it has in its offering. If drug pushing is your forte, your mindset will be different in dealing with your users than that of a real estate salesperson, who also hopes to see a steady flow of new customers, with guaranteed repeat business.

The world is in an avalanche of no-fault extirpations and "ain't my fault" paperwork. The salesman's smile becomes reptilian. In contrast, you want your customers to be genuine, real people with real heart-warming stories to take back home in praise of you and your cult. Make it worth their while and start expanding your head-quarters to accommodate the avalanche of customers hungry for the touch of real people.

4.

First protect the margin

Then boost the turnover. The margin is the buffer for learning lessons and making mistakes. It necessitates the ability to sell on quality. It rewards the bottom line.

Margin protection is the one principle that most marketing strategies and marketing textbooks tend to miss. The economic thought, ever so unscientific, is that falling prices will result in higher sales, as if this is some force of nature and as if economics is a real science.

This is not so. Value is an ephemeral concept, defined in the customer's mind by your unstinting effort, aided by a mega host of competitors. Your customer will equate a witches' brew of emotions, prejudicial mumbo-jumbo and hard-wired, hormonally-influenced pseudo-thoughts into a single: "Yes, mine!", or "Over my dead body! Never! Go away!"

Chomsky said it best: "Business consists of selling goods and services to irrational people making uninformed decisions." A focus on price is dangerous. It ratchets down, never up.

Margin is all-important. If something has to cave into margin protection, it must be cost. Margin is *the* most important part of your business over which to go to war, to make sacrifices and to break down into reinvention.

There can be no heavenly dew sprinkling on the soft cheeks of success in her growing years without adequate, growing, margins. Mistakes can be absorbed when you've got margins. A margin allows emergency cash to be generated. It provides bargaining room and it is oxygen and sustenance in a business. It allows spa-time for tired ideas, infusions of lifeblood, because you can pay for it, as long as your costs are curtailed and in check.

Your margin is your lifeblood – the decisive factor when choosing between those siblings you must sacrifice and those ventures which will get the go-ahead. Without proper and industry-beating margins, the bells will toll and the gravediggers will gather to inter the idiocies of price-cutters, preserving the quality-enhancers. Beware.

5.

CASH! CASH! CASH!

In Business School, the mantra of gearing is preached as if the world is linear and is an accountants' paradise. A great many CEOs are shot up through the financial chute. Many of them are financial engineers, who love to apply money while weaving and bobbing through an uncertain world, a fast-changing industry, in the face of unpredictable responses from suppliers, customers and the competition.

My mantra is cash. I like to end up with enough cash to maintain quarterly dividends at an 8% yield, with three months' worth of turnover in cash and the future well-financed in terms of expansion through product development or market-share expansion.

My approach does mean that the enterprise could have grown faster. My response to this is: "Maybe?" It may look like I plan to go to the beach with inflatables, a ducky tube and diving gear. The reality is that the shark nets are in place, lifeguards are paid for and now we can swim with the dolphins, at speed.

The buffer, safety and anti-ulcer effect of great cash generation are sometimes tarnished as symptoms of a Lazy Balance Sheet. Tell that to Apple and Google, and then again to GM and Ford. The latter two crawled for bailouts, while the first pair understood the world of business.

Cash generation is a product of margin, cost containment and great control over debtors' days. Secondary factors are: great creditor relations and a complete focus by all your staff on fast execution and delivery, as every day lost means cash lost. This isn't a new principle, but it's one that is so often lost at a crucial point and one which can whip the noose around your neck in a single accounting period.

It is best to have an ongoing loose scrum with your shareholders to ration the return of cash rather than a terse meeting with reluctant and recalcitrant bankers whose priorities remain inscrutable and hostile, at best.

All else just amounts to promises, dreams and delusions of near-cash. Cash is a priority, not finance, not promises, not buffer stock or any other safety mechanisms.

6.

DISTRIBUTION IS 90% OF THE GAME

My time at South African Breweries (SAB) in Johannesburg gave a turbo-boost to the few ideas of management that I had, but it was a handful of years later that SAB cracked the code for growth, even though they had effectively been the 'temporary sole-supplier' of beer in South Africa for many years. They had deserved their virtual monopoly. They were that good.

I suspect they became a world-force though the application of what hindsight now tells us was an obvious strategy, hidden in the blind spot of established best practice.

A man will ask for a nice, cold beer … only if it is on offer! Your offering has to be on-hand for your potential customer. If not, he will choose whatever else is available, notwithstanding any of your other efforts.

You need to get it to him. In the rural bush. Under trees. Or at *shebeens* (African informal taverns). It must be on sale where he lives and not just where you offloaded in bulk from your big truck. You need to get down to pick-up level, on barren tracks.

With this understanding, SAB conquered Miller, South America and Eastern Europe. They kept their focus not only on price, quality or operations, but primarily they concentrated on getting the best system for distribution to potential customers. I saw at first hand a family business trucking unheard-of quantities of beer to Groblersdal, a speck on the map. No-one before had bothered to determine the appetite of distribution-neglected, thirst-plagued people.

The same goes for *your* offering. If it is not offered, it can't be chosen. Distribute, and listen to how the distributors want to buy the product. They need to sell it too.

7.

ALWAYS, ALWAYS, FOCUS ON IMPROVING YOUR VALUE-ADDS

The desire to be *the best* is, without fail is on every vision/mission/ ethos scribble I have ever seen. It begets the question of how do you define *the best*? This is answered in two words: best-chosen. We humans are a bag of bacteria masquerading as God's finest on the day He was close to a humour failure. We are not rational, yet we rationalise every decision.

Value-adds must have distinguishing, perceived-value, factors in the eyes of the target market. We make emotional decisions without being in control of our emotions. We are persuaded by fear more than by satisfaction, three times more. We are, at best, unguided missiles in the decision-making process, often making purchase decisions where we choose **safe** over **wow!**

In contrast, your sales force is rational, motivated, guided and loaded.

How will they set your offering apart, to drag the prospect from his current affiliation? He chose the other lot the last time and he did not get fired for that choice.

That's where your lifelong obsession with value-adds must come in. Everyone just loves getting a little extra, a little more, a some-thing-for-nothing. The toy in the cereal box. The importance is not just in what you are offering but the fact that you are tapping into this same vein to get their attention. Value-adds are the most impor-tant way of getting their attention and often are the most effective and cheapest way of turning it into sales bliss.

The easy value-adds hinge on price and promotions. These fade and the market share gained is costly. Put on your customer's shoes and walk that mile. Swop them for your own slippers and leisurely think through your offerings.

At TeleMasters, where we sell telecoms services, we pitched an idea 18 years ago that no-one in our industry has yet dared to consider as no-one we compete with wants to be a follower. We put out a guarantee on price: that we will always beat the market incumbent and we will print a cheque every month for every customer, showing exactly how much cheaper our calls were when compared to the calls of our competitors.

We expanded that to an uptime guarantee. If we can't successfully connect 95% of all calls, it's goodbye to our contract. These examples show what long-lasting value-add looks like. They not only distinguish you from the others; they park that value-add firmly in your corner, perhaps forever.

Next we gave a voice clarity guarantee. The list keeps growing … All of this distinguishes us on the two fronts which are most important in the phone game: quality and price. Your value-adds must be specific. Deliver on Saturdays. Try my product with no obligation for 90-days (we have that one too!). The amount of time put into creating value-adds will help you focus on what the customer wants, but does not yet know that he wants!

Businesses without value-adds are 'me too' businesses and are destined for the scrapheap in any price war. Package your offering differently. Forget credit checks. Draw up a one-page contract. You guessed it; also ours. Offer 24-hour installation instead of the competitors' six weeks. It took us four years to work out the details of that one and to get it done. Surprise and delight the people who want to do business with you, but who couldn't tell their boss before why they chose you. Value-adds can pull it through.

8.

THE MOST LIMITING TYPE OF BUSINESS INVOLVES SELLING EXPERT TIME

It is a second-best approach to have the expertise you sell as your product. Making your business produce an annuity-based income is the way to go and you will gain the first prize, with a distinction, if you can structure it so that the annuity income escalates automatically.

Supplying telecoms solutions is a very rewarding business. It's a growing annuity business that escalates and allows for add-ons to satisfied customers. It's not unique in its structure, but it's a good choice, as you don't need to win a fresh set of customers every month.

How can your business move towards securing an annuity income stream if it's not yet there? Can you add a small support fee that covers all support, instead of charging by incident? How about offering a priority fee that guarantees that your first response will be within 15 minutes, at all hours? Here again is the opportunity for value-adds that the customer will see and accept as making your offering more valuable than the price they are being charged.

Demonstrate to the customer the bargain he is getting. Compare it to scenarios of competitors. Many software companies have moved their business models towards renting their services, rather than the outright purchase of a product. This smooths out the income stream, but it is a hotbed for lazy selling. So perk-up and manage the targets here.

How can the offering be structured to be self-funding if the annuity approach won't fly in your business? If you're an airline company, for example? How can potential passengers be wooed to choose you when they fly? Such opportunities go begging in a world obsessed by price and image and without the understanding of possible self-funding models.

9.

THE BEST FORM OF BUSINESS IS A SUSTAINABLE BUSINESS

Isn't this obvious? Then remember the revolutionary evolutionary Erasmus Darwin, who postulated that each slight variation, if useful, is preserved. Hence, the most-adapted survives the best.

How are you measuring the slight changes in usefulness each day? Are you generating success from your never-ending improvement programmes? Do you actually have any?

The changes of positive adaptation are much slimmer than those from maladaptation and both are subtle. From time to time a new species appears, hopefully from your lab. If not, even the newest creatures, and especially the newest, are in need of modifications to enhance their purpose. This is how a sustainable business is sustained, through trial and foolish error, trial and small success. In all areas.

It seems the term 'sustainable' has been appropriated to mean a *green* business, as if business should only be beholden to a philosophy of 'reduce, re-use and recycle'. Perhaps this is a small step. Businesses should follow the laws of nature by not wasting and not exerting unneeded effort, by being efficient and collaborative, through being reciprocally useful to the host and the prey.

Few folk hail from farms these days. Fewer CEOs, therefore, have a deep understanding of the cycles, of birth, of inevitable death and the symbioses of nature. One law is: putting in before taking out. Another is: leaving something behind for the next round. The list goes on … If you can understand the cruel but necessary laws here, your understanding of both the meanings of sustainable will surely help inform your decisions.

Life is a great sifting process and you are in the winnowing wind in all aspect of your life – in business, in home life, in tennis games and in every conversation. Go with the flow. Domination is your middle name, but live a sustainable life with your sustainable business.

Foes don't need to be vanquished. The time of swords, with seconds at daybreak, has gone. It's best you apply your considerable skills to turn opposition into support. Making friends of those who remind us too much of ourselves is a challenge worthy of your rank, and the happy result will be a high point indeed. That will be a superb example of symbiosis, a very valuable form of sustainability.

10.

Hate all surprises, even the good ones. Anticipate events. Plan around them

Testosterone and cortisol enhance and destroy the lives of those under stress. Surprises are an example of those unwanted spikes that usually ratchet up the heart-affecting baddies.

The Risk List is an unheralded tool. It should be updated often, involving many different people in the organisation. This is the Bad Surprise list, where no contingency exists, chaos may ensue and your carefully-crafted seamless mantra of Great Leader may be shredded in a moment if you cannot pull the proverbial rabbit from the headgear.

For a long time, we took reliable electricity supply for granted in South Africa. It was on no-one's risk list. Six years of often-intermittent supply has made us appreciate even more those days when there is consistent electricity supply.

Businesses in South Africa now don't just need generators to cover power failures, but also need PC profile back-ups of every user, just in case the customer's office is burgled and cleaned out. Everyone can be up-and-running within the hour, as a financing line has been pre-approved to purchase new laptops, plus software, and all profiles, including stored e-mails, will be pushed from the remote cloud location.

The risk list carries on. Which customers, if unhappy, will dent your reputation? Or worse, your cash flow? Manage the surprise. Which employees, if head-hunted, will take undocumented intellectual property (IP) along? What are the doomsday scenarios? Are there plans in place and have these plans been tested? What about a tax authority raid, when they might leave with the server, saying they are taking it to look for evidence? How do you react to a competitor alleging criminal intent? How would you cope with the death or sudden disability of those in key positions?

Good surprises denote uninformed leadership or, at worst, unmanaged expectations. What's the best news expected this week? How can it be a surprise then? Make it a policy of knowing what's coming. That's the way to keep the testosterone levels level and unimpeded, like you intended to. In fact, define you role in two words: no surprises.

11.

CAN YOU SELL IN SIX WORDS OR LESS YOUR FIRM'S REASON FOR EXISTENCE, GOAL AND ADVANTAGE?

This sounds difficult, but it's a fair challenge: sell your advantage over the competition in six words or less. It's the elevator speech in a one-floor ride. It's the answer to: "Why should we choose you?" It's not: "What do you sell?" The first denotes a benefit of note in the context of an offering.

Imagine a missionary stepping off the boat. After three steps into the jungle he finds his first prospect, who sticks a spear under his chin.

He is asked: "Why are you here?"
He replies: "I've come to make converts from heathens like you for my church."
The response is: "Why should I join? You have three words left."
This is a wonderful opportunity, but failure means death. It is an example that I love to use.
The priest says: "Go to Heaven."
The response: "If I don't?"
The Holy Man suggests: "Go to …"

You knew this answer. Now the priest can expand on what Heaven is, how to get there, the awfulness of a bad choice. Later he can teach his tormentor to read, to translate the Good Book into the native language, to build a church and so on. His short speech sold the oldest, and probably the most successful, organisation since the Roman Empire.

Who are you? In six words or less. Can you encapsulate your way of living in the same way? Why you chose and married her, from an array of available beauties?

Keep your thoughts succinct on this. You will have to sell your saliva-inducing concept hundreds of times to your peers. You want their instant respect for your acumen, as well as their business, as soon as possible.

This approach makes it easy for your front-liners and their spouses to answer that pertinent question: "Why are you working at X?" Without an enthusiastic answer, what meaning would their professional lives have, other than the drudgery of slave labour in a place where no-one can spell out their worth? The same is true for the rest of your staff and also includes their kids: "Daddy works at X, where they make people go to Heaven. That's a cool place." Imagine how your reputation will spread. Or, if not, Hell is where it won't.

12.

WHAT ARE THE TEN (OR FEWER) PRINCIPLES GOVERNING YOUR STAFF'S ACTIONS TOWARDS GLORY?

Are you able to express your philosophy towards your business and all those connected to it in a few pertinent, memorable sentences without sounding like a public relations alien who is fluent only in marketing speak?

Are the principles unwaveringly accepted as being fixed and fair?

Fewer principles are better than too many. My favourite is the Viking creed: "Do what is right and fear no-one." It's persuasive, moral and impressively succinct, too.

In the context of an organisation, it may be expanded a bit, for illustrative purposes only. Let me tell you what TeleMasters hammered-out 15 years ago. It is neither extensive, nor all-encompassing, nor a manual to Measure Everything By. It is a reminder of my unconventional, but workable, approach to doing business.

Our TeleMasters principles are:
1. CANI: Constant And Never-ending Improvement
2. No Mistakes: Fix and learn, or risk getting booted out
3. Excellence only in RESULTS: No excellence in unproductive effort
4. Values AND Performance: Fitting into the culture AND delivering the expected performance
5. Do it TODAY: Time-management and focus on completion
6. Long-term Relationships: For customers and employees alike

7. Measure and Report: Everything, viewable by everyone; all participate daily
8. Responsibility and Accountability: Match between tasks and authority
9. Unconsciously Competent: Last stage up from unconsciously incompetent
10. CASH is KING: No substitutes

Ever so often, we discuss and finger-point these, but our principles have remained the same for the last decade. Staffers know these off by heart, and their boo-boos are measured against them. What's displayed in your reception area?

13.

THERE ARE TWO DIRECTIONS OF INNOVATION: PRODUCT INNOVATION (EXPENSIVE AND DIFFICULT) AND PROCESS INNOVATION (MUCH CHEAPER AND EASIER)

Everything can be improved through Process Innovation. This is the easy, Darwinian way. TeleMasters' largest 'ah-ha!' and leap in processes were when we figured out – idiots that we had been before – that there are two approaches. You can deal with things in series, or with things in parallel. We changed as much as we could to the parallel approach and we now start several processes at once when we receive an order.

The fact-checking starts simultaneously with the system-profile creation and the product set-ups. The technical planning starts at the same moment. Within a day, everything is ready to roll. No-one waits on anyone else to get started. Once the last of the processes has been finished, installation begins. This cuts the execution time for a job from weeks to hours.

From time to time, admin nixed the customer, or the tech department found terminal problems with a specific site. The abandonments and wasted efforts were miniscule when compared to the benefit and confidence gained by the gang approach.

So how long does it take to receive a new passport? What would happen if everything was done in parallel? Or my favourite bugbear: the three-week waiting list. Imagine if extra effort was made to catch-up and the goodies appeared from the machine in the time it took to make them?

Process Innovation brings permanent benefits. There is a world of ways to do things better – if they need to be done at all. At TeleMasters, we abandoned the entire customer credit-checking procedure a decade ago. The delay this had caused was usually two weeks. The information would have been out of date in a month, perhaps less. The cost and effort of keeping all customers' details updated would be prohibitive. So we charged a month's use upfront and in this way we covered our risk.

Processes are the lifeblood but when things get snarled up, just like when blood clots form in the vein, they can also be deadly obstacles. Spend some time in every department, watching what they do and how they do it. Then you may understand the approach: "I must create work, or else I could be fired." The inefficiency, the drudgery, the unnecessary tasks, the compliance fears and, worst of all, the showing up of a Jurassic and flawed methodology. All this will drive you to tears. The inane e-mails, the excuses for repeating an ineffective procedure: herein lies the great maw of unnecessary cost in time and money.

Think through the process of keeping a customer informed and happy. Plan around them and then relentlessly cut down the steps and ANY 'pass-along-to-Fred' practices for the step that comes next. Keep responsibility for the entire process with a single person, but double up the people, in parallel. Sniff out the delays and time the executions.

Now you will be able to find time for the magic of Product Innovation.

You may eventually want to choose between Product Innovation and Process Innovation. Don't. Choose both.

14.

WHAT ARE THE LIMITS OF ACCEPTABLE MEASURED OUTCOMES? WHY?

What would *stun* you if it dramatically improved? Debtors' days down to 16 days? Turnaround time at 48 hours?

Any challenge to the helmsman of your vessel work like a double-edged sword. We all respond well to incentives and adversely to criticism. We also take for granted what is possible with minimal effort and often set the outcomes based on this.

Suddenly a 12-year-old Girl Scout sells a record number of cookies and there are sheepish looks on the faces of your ever-so-professional sales staff.

It is always good to constantly recalibrate expectations. What target would be stunning and extremely beneficial if it could be reached consistently?

How about bringing debtors' days down to 16 days? Working in an industry with a 65-day average, TeleMasters maintains 12 debtors' days. We set this knockout goal and figured the **how**, through bank debit orders and one month's prepaid usage. Strangely, no-one in the industry followed us. We were branded as lucky.

What if you could offer a turnaround time of less than six weeks for fixed-line installations? We got it down to 24 hours. We also made a major breakthrough when we found a way to converge mobile bandwidth with fixed-line services.

Your enterprise may also have an array of traditional practices in place. They were put in place before your time, following strategies and ideas from the days of yore. Now is the time to make the blood rise and to stiffen the sinews for the jump. What will stun the people in your enterprise and your competitors?

The confidence of your cadres will be much improved if you can pull this off. Note that this is not an exhortation to extra effort, but a clever and cunning way to rethink the possible and find a way around it. Accept no limits, only accolades.

15.

HALF OF YOUR EFFORTS TOWARDS THE OUTSIDE WORLD SHOULD ENAMOUR YOUR TARGET MARKET

THE OTHER HALF SHOULD SCARE THE PANTS OFF YOUR COMPETITORS. DON'T FAIL IN EITHER

Talking to the competition is difficult, if not downright illegal in some countries. Nonetheless, you should accept that your secrets and goings-on are leaking like a sieve through the tech department. People who are predominantly left-brained – and this may be a classification myth – tend to share their common interest easier with other techies. No wonder they are so non-garrulous at the office.

This is the ideal channel to get word out to the market. Always include as many of the staff as possible when describing the details of your new assaults. People need to share the excitement with their spouses. What could it mean to their careers and their corporate prospects? Spouses then need to drop the word at social gatherings.

You need to pitch the 'New and Improved!' version of your business with two audiences in mind: your esteemed customers and your irreverent opposition.

Sometimes things do not work out so well on the money interface. The offering needs an overhaul, an adaptation, as noted before. However, the spectre of doom must be ingrained in any opponent who reads between the lines and concludes of your new and improved model: "If this works, we're all toast." Or something that at least gets them thinking and staying up at night.

Your innovations and restructured benefits will be unique for a while. If they are sufficiently disseminated amongst the opposition you may find that there is little appetite to imitate. They have egos too. The field is secure for a while and you may have an unopposed run. Until Darwin next strikes.

16.

CHOOSE QUALITY OVER QUANTITY

It is a slow but satisfying progression from quality to quantity, but a hazardous one the other way.

The best watch in the world is not necessarily the most expensive. Nowadays, people can hardly compute value from the elements of quality and price. Incessant brand-marketing has led to consumers, as well as the people who staff your customers' decision-making departments, to mistake price for quality. This is not necessarily a bad thing if you are in the quality business. The claim can be backed up, usually by direct comparison with the rest of the vendors on the shopping list.

Quality should not be a foggy concept. It is decidedly mundane if you define it yourself. Heaven help the telecoms executive who is asked by his customer: "How good is the voice quality on your network?" This means that neither party has so pertinently defined the ratios or elements of quality in a manner which the customer can confirm, in an intelligent way, so that he can assess that the quality is, indeed, superb.

Very, very, few CEOs take the trouble to define quality in the mind of their prospect. Measurement of Service (MoS) is a rating on a five-point scale that defines voice quality in telecoms, but no customer can measure it. Therefore, we would instead educate him about hiss, warble, connection delays and volume, all which are absent in our brand of digital communications. Most other VoIP systems have these non-lethal, but customer-killing, deficiencies. It may not surprise you that we keep telling our customers that.

What's the best-quality printer? Your guess. Watch? Automobile? Widget? Unless you can define quality, there will be limited acceptance. Once defined on your own terms, and hopefully tangibly, it is easier to sell quality. Then improve your offering to reflect more and better quality, on your own terms, to differentiate your offering more.

If your quality acceptance path is going well, you have all the impetus needed to push quantity, and probably at a superior price to that of the quantity-only purveyor.

17.

A 'QUALITY' SELL IS MUCH MORE LUCRATIVE THAN A SALE BASED ON DISCOUNT

It's an old adage that if you give your salespeople the discretion to discount, they will do exactly that. So don't. You have a quality product with many enhancements, supported extremely well. Of course it also never breaks down, but just in case it does … Your sales guys have a proper intro and the elevator speech, understand the choices in the market and are primed to build life-long relationships.

You shouldn't aim just to make a customer happy, but you should aim to find how you can improve his world. Just being happy? That feeling may come from a botched sale and a fat discount, and you want to offer so much more … Real improvement comes from filling a gap that the customer didn't know you could fill so well, and maybe never knew existed in the first place.

A sale is a transaction of value. If no effort of effective execution, of translating that value, takes place, then either you have the wrong customer at the wrong time, or the wrong approach is being taken by your representative. It takes performance, and this is what is so expected of you, to lay the foundation of trust. The consideration to change will only come after trust has been won.

The performance is the key. By now you might have seen a number of good plays for the same entry fee, and some were more satisfying than others. Your salesperson is singing for his supper and he must ensure the customer is in the mood (market) to hear his performance (sales pitch).

A quality sale is not a one-way street, or a rattling-off of features, benefits, comparisons, PowerPoints, or glossy brochures. It is a dialogue with questions, pointed answers, illumination, options, interaction, and, at last, the conclusion. Trust.

Are we there? Propose now, not before. Only with confidence can the quality sale takes place, instilling confidence in your organisation, your actor and your product, as well as the confidence exuded by that actor. It should be a harbinger of the future relationship. We'll meet often in future and every time will be an experience that will reinforce why it was so clever and fruitful to choose us.

Price is secondary. Any customer demanding a good discount upfront needs even more tender ministrations to form relationships, instead of unfulfilling one-night stands based on price.

18.

NEVER GET ATTACHED TO YOUR ASSETS. GET ATTACHED TO YOUR CASH

Is this only a phrase, or is it a proper business concept? The day your cash is in a headlock, you may remember it. Call me old-fashioned, but I am wary, apprehensive and downright allergic to leverage. Life is uncertain, business more so and temptations conspire against us on a daily basis, disguised as blue-eyed, loving deals. Cash is the buffer.

One of our seemingly trite principles is: Cash is King. This underpins a deeper philosophy of business, which says that the true measure of business success is in the size of dividends you distribute. On our bourse, the Johannesburg's Stock Exchange, TeleMasters is presently the only company that pays quarterly dividends. We pay those dividends *before* the end of every quarter. Of course, we know our cash position on a daily basis. It helps with the accounting, too.

This means we need to prove our acumen in cash terms. We keep at least six months' worth of overheads in accessible cash and there were times we needed that access during a transition phase to new technology. We could self-fund the transition, ride it out and get into a higher gear once it was successfully implemented.

As CEO, I believe that the six-month forecast of cash is a daily metric that must be studied, planned around and vigorously tested and verified. Achieving a stable forecast and a satisfactory level of operating and risk funds will greatly enhance the sleeping patterns of owners and management alike.

At the same time, you may note from the financial statements of your opposition that they may not be so intent on gathering like the ant and may instead show grasshopper tendencies. This makes your opposition vulnerable to a swoop on their best salesperson, the undercutting of the price to their largest customer and the foisting of all manner of Hell on their deliveries if you can secure sole-supplier status with their vendors.

In such situations, many fortunes are made and the weak are exploited mercilessly by the strong. It's the way of all nature. Stock, debtors, fancy furniture? None of these is cash. Cash is your ally. Not assets. Get attached to it and stay attached to it.

19.

TIMING IS EVERYTHING. TIMING THE BUY IS EXPONENTIALLY EASIER THAN TIMING THE SELL

The market is a moving target. Your customers are subject to their biorhythms, to bonus cycles, competition and internal politics. Timing a buy is a delicate and exquisite science, and the amateur is most assuredly upstaged by the professional. The deciding factors in the purchase are the options, the competition, and what the competition has and knows about your options.

Buying is easier than selling, as you have the power of cash. The other party can do infinite things with money, while your options with the item or company being purchased are limited. Likewise, the power moves to the buyer when you are the owner of the limited-use thing on offer. Your effort at the sale is the dance between buyers, more victim than hunter.

This is where time and timing can be your strength as a buyer. You may cajole, entice, bamboozle and threaten the seller, while keeping the other bidders at bay. You know full-well that the seller is doing his best to step away from an emotional decision into a rational one, based on price and the right terms. Meanwhile, he knows that you need to be wooed on the advantages, suitability and necessity of swopping cash for goods.

Thus, the timing of your decisions influences the price, as you may promise ease of transaction before pricing, and may demand increased assurances before commitment. As a seller, you are at a great disadvantage in dealing with a well-versed buyer. Doubly so, if he can determine the time and timing limits that constrain you.

Timing is *everything*. It would be fatal to move too early, or too late. Get in touch with the rhythms of your industry.

The hunt for viable options is paramount before you launch the process of the buy, or the sell. He who has the best options available can make the best decision. Never sell, or buy, yourself short when hunting for the bargain, or putting your item up for sale.

20.

PLANT SEEDS FOR TREES AND FOR VEGETABLES

In farming, trees yield more than annuals per hectare. Yet they take longer to produce their bounty, which some may see as a deficit in a fast-changing, result-hungry world. Once vines are established, at considerable cost, the grapes grow season after season and requires much less time and effort than at the establishment. Olive trees may still yield after a thousand years. Trees eventually take less time and effort than vegetables.

This is how customers and offerings must be graded. Your hunters are constantly sowing seeds. Their choice of mix determines the firm's ultimate success. Customer business that can be classified as 'vegetables' is characterised by small orders, easily won. However, it takes a lot of nutritious veg to feed the organisation. Each customer-cycle needs a repeat of the same process and this can be burdensome.

Higher-value customers may take much longer to wean off their current supplier and to establish firmly as a tree. The bigger the customer, the longer the sales-cycle and the more people, resources and effort is needed. In the wooing phase, no monies flow, margins aren't made and no commissions are paid. There is a golden mean between short-term veg and long-term trees right now. It will change in future, and you want to end up with many more trees.

Getting this wrong has obvious consequences. The onset of frost may kill off the small plants, although having too few trees will curtail the firm's growth. Too much focus on obtaining trees may stress the cash flow and may demoralise your front-liners.

The secret is to sow widely, and to choose carefully. Some customers are not worth having. At TeleMasters, we regard lawyers and call centres businesses with well-founded suspicion on timely payments. Anyone in a hurry, or feigning importance, will fall off the prospects list. Enthusiastic customers raise serious suspicion, there is no place for unbridled emotion with us. Conservative industries are trees that grow far too slowly for our sales-cycles. Franchises are low-yield vegetables, while owner-run businesses are a top priority. Take time to understand your flora and your diet.

21.

DISTINGUISH BETWEEN EVENTS AND PATTERNS

We all hate excuses. We all hate disappointments and failures. We need to classify these as either events or patterns in order to make an appropriate assessment of their meaning.

The one-offs may be excused when there is no malice attached. It's the second appearance of a similar incident which should sound the air-raid sirens all over. If it's not malicious, at least the turning of events into patterns denotes a habit of sorts. Someone is hacking at the system, or someone is playing truant with the truth. One event may be forgiven, but the emergence of a pattern must be detected and resisted, with a fury.

Patterns may emerge from condoned events. Even when condoned, the taproot must be firmly cut off to stop any subsequent proliferation of the unwanted plant. Too often our understanding and empathy are misunderstood as a blanket acceptance of something which has gone off-track. Any subsequent firmness against a practice which was unwanted, but was forgiven just once, may raise the temperature all round.

A single incident of accidental trespassing cannot and should not be waived away as an honest mistake. Time and effort must be taken to explain the consequences of trespassing, treating it as if it had been done deliberately and provocatively. The impression of a suspended sentence must be imprinted. Hopefully this will establish the boundaries for all within earshot or in the grapevine: that rules are not applicable *only* from the second try. It is a no-tolerance world and ignorance and happenstance may be excused only after the proper implications are detailed and understood.

Fire people for making deliberate or uncorrected major mistakes. Reward them for ably corrected major mistakes, as that's where learning and experience will stem from.

Does all this sound a little harsh? Perhaps. So the message should be cloaked in sweetness and in light, while resolute and unbending in its underlying substance.

22.

DISTINGUISH BETWEEN 'CAUSE' AND 'EFFECT'

Many of us are familiar with the herringbone method of finding the real cause of a situation. I have never, ever, seen it in practice, but there may be wise CEOs who use this approach and come to real, intelligent conclusions.

A distinction must always be made between what seems to be the cause and what *really drives* that cause. Without an understanding of primary causes, your calculations and projections will be off the beam.

Why do your debtor collections peak close to the 25th of every month? Is that when creditors like to pay, or is that when the Debtor Department gets insistent on payment and thereby unnecessarily raises the stakes or sours the relationship?

Why does a competitor lower his prices? Is it because he is gunning for market share, or is he in an overstock/under-cash situation?

Why do you have difficulty in getting good salespeople? Is it true what your Sales Director says? That you pay too little? Or is it his poor reputation in the market that keeps away the high-fliers?

It is difficult and treacherous to find the true answers. These may change at a moment's notice, too. Still, it is imperative that you challenge the clichés and the established wisdoms, which masquerade as easy excuses for a broken system.

Don't confuse the symptom with the cause. Don't blame Rasputin. Without the weak-willed Czar, the Romanovs might still be around. Any parasite can grow in a supportive environment.

Often, the effects are mislabelled as causes. A bit of your trained mind should disperse this, but you will still have to ask questions to which, like any decent lawyer, you already know the answers.

Sometimes you hear the complaint: "We can't get finance because our net assets are too low." Well, that is not a cause. It is the effect of not getting debtors' days down to 15, at which point you would not need the finance. The real cause may be the inability of the people who deal with your debtors/customers to influence the margins at which your offerings are sold, leaving no room for settlement discounts at the initial payment time.

23.

FEED THE INNOVATION LEAKAGE FUND

Leak a little gambling money on the new, and maybe exciting, things.

How much does innovation cost? The answer is not only: "Who knows?" It's also: "It depends ..." Had you known exactly what to fund, and when, you would be enjoying astronomical and galactic returns for having pushed the right button at the right time.

For most of the time, innovation expansion, with new methods and processes, is decidedly hit and miss. The success rate is not encouraging. The Edison myth of 10 000 failures resounds even worse if you look at what *really* happened. He stole Joseph Swann's 10-year-old patent and later William Sawyer's. The light bulb was never his invention. Still he didn't stop trying ...

Innovation is unpredictable. It's best that you set aside some money to encourage it. You will have to bleed some funds intelligently, without any guaranteed return. This is your venture fund; a commitment to encourage innovation and thinking.

Think like a farmer. There's equipment preparation, soil preparation, planting, fertilising, herbicide and insecticide spraying, weather-watching and praying, more tilling, weeding and leaf nutrient application. This is for a generally well-known process. For a while, nothing happens. Whatever comes up may be random as well. Who knows what will grow, or how well it will grow, if you prep and plant? Aim to get your thumbs green.

Your industry and your risk profile will be indicative of the size of your visible commitment to the future.

Do payments to consultants also fall into this category? Isn't that a great topic for debate?

24.

UNDERSTAND AND CALCULATE THE LIFETIME VALUE OF EACH CUSTOMER'S BUSINESS. PROTECT AND ENHANCE IT

You are already familiar with big numbers. Here's a way to exercise that capability … What will your ten best customers be worth after 20 years: assuming an annual sales growth of 5%, with margin improvement of 5% and present value at a 3% discount?

Now, calculate how much that is worth per hour, from now to then, and how much you are getting paid for those hours. Perhaps it would be a good investment to go to see them rather more regularly, say every three months. Determine how much they would have accumulated for your benefit in that period, and how much it would cost you in time and effort to spend an hour with each of them. It is assuredly an incredible return on investment.

Some believe that it is far easier to sell more to a new customer. Others opine that it is also much cheaper to service an existing account than to get a new one.

Common sense counters that your customer is yours for the losing. Make him happy and loyal, and keep him that way, and it will be a bulwark against the frustrated competition. You will have a valued name on your reference list.

If you love your customer, how are you showing it? By sending a monthly black-and-white demand of: "Pay me, or else …!" Is that your most frequent customer contact?

Our invoices start with: "Our esteemed Customer XXX …"

Each ends with an eight page, full-colour, graphic-rich analysis of his entire usage in the previous month, showing trends and other useful information.

First we show the most important part: a cheque with the exact amount that our services saved him, in comparison to what he was being charged by his previous supplier.

We validate our promise every month, without fail. If you the customer make no savings, we lose the contract.

Members of our debtors' team are called Customer Relationship Managers (CRMs). They tend to talk to the customers more than anyone else. They get to see the good customers, as well as the recalcitrant ones.

Then we have the *melktert* strategy. The melktert, or milk tart, is a typical *Boere* pie, served with coffee. It has a little dusting of cinnamon and it is delicious.

Our CRMs and salespeople pack a *melktert* for each visit to the Great and to the Horrible.

The first questions, face-to-face, with an important non-paying customer are always: "What did we do wrong? You used to pay us. So did we screw up something recently? We're extremely sorry. Let's share the *melktert* … Tell us about it and then we can fix it."

No confrontation. Just 'people-buy-from-people' affirmation of the importance to us of the relationship. Our debtors' days have been hovering at around 12 for the last decade. Each *melktert* costs about USD$2.00. Go figure *that* investment.

25.

Yes, people are generally lazy, ignorant and stupid most of the time. So make it easy, informative and clever to choose your offering

That applies to you as well. You want something and you choose the prospective vendors based on reputation or reference. The warm bodies pitch their wares, after which you make your emotional decision based on …? Well, then you justify it, factually. It's called rationalising your decision, and that is how humans are wired to do it.

If you ever doubt that we are generally incapable of *ever* getting even the most important decision correct, just look at the choice of spouse made by those around you. It's worse for men, too. There's no make-up to conceal our blemishes. No 'come-on' moves … You get the idea?

So there's a grim-faced, tight-lipped, unknown person hiding behind a blank façade and wire-rimmed glasses, watching your performance for the first time.

This is no different to being the actor on stage. The audience is unknown, but they paid for entry. Your prospect took an hour of his busy life and invited you to his boardroom. He has paid the price and now it's up to you.

Always validate the other person in your very first sentence. Of course you've Googled the company and read their press releases. You have read his LinkedIn profile. You know who his current supplier is, what their weaknesses are. Within the first seconds of introduction, you need to connect to this possibly ignorant and uninformed, but smart, stranger.

Validate. It's personal, so I can offer no pointers here. Your sincerity and the relevance of the comment is the difference between isometrics and progress. Isometrics makes you tired but gets you nowhere. "Pleased to meet you, John. You're the guy that spoke so well on biometrics at Langley last year?" That's validation! And so on.

Get to the easy, informative and relevant. It's hard hunting on the savannahs of Africa. Your forebears did this and now it's time for you to do this for the benefit of your progeny. You have a willing participant as prey. Except that you want to be seen to give more than you want to take away. Make this the best hour of his life. Of course you are prepared and decisive, informed and rational.

Etch the performance into John's memory, as you should do with almost everyone outside of your company. They lead boring and stressful lives of limited meaning and you could be the one to add warmth with their clever purchase from your crowd.

26.

PREACH THE 100% WORLD

My darling eldest daughter, who is 12, boasted of her 93% maths-test score. "Great, Isabella," I replied, "but what would happen if Dr Lumart lost 7% of his patients? Or if Daddy missed only 93% of all the cars on the road, driving to the farm?"

Many parents condemn me at this point for being too hard on the child and blunting her spirit. Really?

Well, how many mistakes are allowed in the General Ledger before you lose your patience? What if Diana decides to call on only 93% of her overdue customers? Or Joyce ignores only 7% of the calls at the switchboard? It's a 100%, no-mistake, reality in the world of business.

Some parents are happy with a 60% academic average. So the kids have no clue about the importance of other 40%. Happy with this score out of 100, the child grows up, joins the workforce and arrives at work only six days in ten, misses delivery of 40% of his assigned tasks, and is mortified to learn that this is totally unacceptable.

Maybe the problem lies with those parents who accept under-performance from their kids, without realising the damage done to a child's expectations and to his or her performance once out in the real world.

Mistakes occur and we do fire people for making mistakes. A mistake is only an unfixed error. Fixing an error is a learning experience and we applaud that. A 40% mistake-rate leaves so much room for learning, and should never just lead to a shrug of indifference.

Preach the 100% world and stick to your guns. Insubordination is an act of cowardice from someone not convinced that his way is better and without the conviction to state it upfront. All processes are up for debate and should remain so. A contrary view should be heard, debated and cogently dismissed or accepted. Then the task should be 100% implemented. Or else.

27.

THERE IS NO SHORTAGE OF GOOD IDEAS, BUT GOOD PEOPLE ARE RARE. BUILD YOUR BUSINESS AROUND THE GOOD PEOPLE YOU CAN FIND

To put your wonderful and creative mind in perspective, page through the latest issue of the *Patent Journal*, and cringe. There is an average of 60 000 patents approved per month, worldwide. Should these patents be implemented, the world could be reborn at least every 21 days as a new Utopia – on a never-ending basis.

That is never the way things turns out. A miniscule number of ideas will be commercially successful and those, which fail, will be a tragedy of the human spirit and of our dreams for an ever-better future. Why is this?

The obstacles are endless, but predictable. Not only is every new idea supplanting some form of an old idea, but it is also competing for the same resources currently being spent on something similar, or being spent elsewhere.

The best ideas do not necessary win. The 300 mpg car has been built a number of times, but it has been commercially unsuccessful.

What underlies this is the true idiom of venture capitalists: don't bet on the horse; bet on the jockey.

The plan or the man? The man, or woman, is generally the better bet.

Unless you're the top dog of your industry, unlimited in imagination and funds, you would be hard-pushed to find a better strategy for success than to choose your soldiers well and then to build the business around their capabilities. They become your most important Intellectual Asset! They know the vicissitudes of your customers and how to navigate around the weaknesses of your systems and features, until you can fix these.

The best success stories are almost entirely thanks to human talent and endeavour. Such as Jon Ives and Elon Musk, people who navigate the unknowns and make these places commonplace and well-tamed. People buy from people, and people trust people. People want people to sort out their problems. In both the ups and the downs, human interaction is the prime concern. It can add a significant margin to whatever is on the table, be it good news or bad notice. Choose well.

28.

THE STAFF ARE THE KINGS; CHOOSE THEIR SIDE WHEN IN DOUBT

You have many customers and infinitely more potential ones. You have far fewer staff.

This sounds like heresy in an age with the adage that: "The customer is king!" It is repeated as often as the 1940s Kellogg's ploy of: "Breakfast is the most important meal of the day."

Here's my thinking, I hope you agree?

We have 16,000 customers and fewer than a hundred staff serving them. In another business of mine, in the mining sector, we have 350 staff serving 85 customers.

We field three types of calls from customers: account queries, reports of technical difficulties and requests for information. Sometimes they translate into: "Get me the CEO! I need to vent my anger."

I carefully choose, and willingly pay, a number of good people to leave that joyful place called home every weekday, to be incarcerated all the daylight hours. Sitting down and staring at a screen, dealing with a pile of papers and a constantly ringing phone.

There is a special bond between us and they provide the mechanism for the organisation to function, to flower and to pay dividends to all who participate in it. It is a biomass of skills, expertise, smiles and a repository of great wisdom. These people accumulate experiences daily and transmute reluctance into joy in their customer interactions.

Only a select few applicants will ever fit in and make a career with either TeleMasters, SperoSens, or with the other businesses I am involved in.

Customers, on the other hand, are numerous. We choose them and invite them to join our gallery of symbiotic collaborators, but with the unwavering promise that life is too short to deal with nasty people. Scream at my staff once and I, at CEO level, will personally fire you as a customer. Insult my people and you will find yourself at the receiving end of a *crimen injuria* case, never mind who is in the right or in the wrong.

In any 50/50 situation, I will choose the side of my staff. They know it. If I have to make a marginal call, it will be in in their support and I will jettison a customer, if needs be. We often acquire other business and then our people will need to deal with their people. Their people are a reflection of their business ethos, and if the signs on a lower level are not good, then we note this, as we can do without chilling surprises later on.

Mistakes occur. Honesty and factual correctness are needed. If you are in charge, your decision must be unemotional and binding. Be particularly alert to patterns. The same person in your team may have a second and then a third scrap with a customer, but will plead blamelessness. Then you may need to re-evaluate his worth. Still, the confidence you inspire by backing your team is easily worth a handful of customers.

29.

PEOPLE BUY FROM PEOPLE

Sex sells, confidence sells, relationships matter. Yes they do. There are many tags for this, but there are also many fits and misfits. Find different approaches and effective ways to 'unlock' a relationship that is presently frozen.

Your worst ex-customer will find a new supplier. Your best one might find a new one, too. Not necessarily by browsing competitors' sites, but by being mesmerised face-to-face by a persistent person with a wonderful performance and a memorable message. Oops!

Here is the lesson of Katie Francis, the 2014 world-record-setting Girl Scout cookie seller: 18 107 boxes. Beside hard work and a lot of time, she said: "You have to talk to everybody." She was 12 years old. She asked everyone she met to buy some cookies. She got a lot of yeses.

So your sales guys are still playing Lord Almighty by choosing carefully who they talk to, as if the prospective customer can make a decision before you have called on them? How can they assess a prospect unless they get up from their computer, descend on the target, and deliver their stage performance? This is where you want them to act their best performance, in good voice – not playing the laptop keyboard.

Not successful? Use the same message, but with a different face. People like to buy from people they like. Some prospective purchasers may not click with Greg. Then send Moira. Then try Corene. The message will be the same message, but by now the degree of understanding must surely be higher. Build the trust to get the momentum that is needed to seal the deal.

30.

THERE IS NO EXCELLENCE IN EFFORT, ONLY EXCELLENCE IN RESULTS

Of all our TeleMasters business principles, this is the most effective one. It embodies a host of hopes and fears, sacrifices and achievements and became the ultimate arbiter of an individual's worth to the company.

There's shame in the phrase: "I tried." The same extends to all its variants: "I left a message for him." "I couldn't crack that." "I am waiting for her to get back." "We're busy with it." And so on and on.

A directive must be given with a deadline. If it sounds unreasonable to the executor, he should raise his concern there and then and a decision must be made. At the same time, a priority must be assigned. Every time I delegate, it miraculously becomes someone else's top priority, which is unfair to my Business Unit Controller at TeleMasters. Poor Leanie!

Those are the ground rules, and results must follow. Our rule is that if you become stuck on a problem, then that problem needs to be escalated. When the sun sets and the comforts of home are calling you, all tasks must have been completed, or should be in an advanced state of completion, within the deadlines and priorities which have been set. The mundane and the urgent are separated from one another. New tasks and issues may take precedence and disrupt. As the African proverb goes: the grass never stops growing and the cows will never stop eating. So the work is never finished.

Learn from nature: lions never waste effort.

It is imperative that the expectation of the required results being achieved, on time, should be established – firmly and with no scope for re-negotiation. If there is a lapse, you may escalate the task to someone else, with a resultant loss of confidence in the initial underachiever. Thus the pecking order is altered. Egos are at play, too. This internal 'Who's Who' is far stronger than any relationship could be with people you just need to pay every month.

Excellence only. Excellence always. First-time results. This may sound like corporate and enterprise heaven. And it is. Make angels of your people and in this way you will help them to understand their potential and worth.

31.

DISTINGUISH BETWEEN ACHIEVEMENTS AND WORK DONE

Achievements are beyond the call of duty, haven't been done before, and significantly impact on the firm. Reward those achievements. Encourage them, expect them and measure them.

There is no substitute for the self-worth that is fostered when one's achievements are measured, rewarded and commended. Perhaps you should consider a company-wide system of rewarding such achievements.

The basis for this is twofold. First, challenge the would-be Navy Seal on what he will achieve, and when? Then measure this against time expectations and the original intent. Reward over-achievement appropriately through word, deed and public accolade, where appropriate.

This approach should form a cornerstone of your annual, or hopefully more frequent, performance reviews. Performance is enhanced when achievements have been recognised. Of course you should steer aspirations towards those areas in the forest that will yield the best timber to bring home.

Completed tasks are what get paid for. This is the minimum standard of output, the oiling of the gears and the tuning of the engine. It is the achievements beyond the expected and the required that stand out; and they may not necessarily be related to the employee's position or job description. The Tech Manager wants to do a monthly Tech Update Newsletter? Yip.

Someone else wants to re-organise the storeroom to the efficiency of a Formula One pit stop? That sounds good, too. Elevate their expectations and cultivate their confidence. How on earth will you resist the expectation of a salary increase when you know that you received far more value from this person?

Eliminate the pre-work syndrome. The 'preparation-for', the 'trying-to-do', the 'getting-ready' and the 'waiting-for' viruses are deadly and contagious. How much action can you expect from an average office worker? Four hours per day? The rest may be taken up by e-mails and interruptions. Set them straight on what's expected by noon. Then the rest of their day is not your concern, but is their opportunity for acquiring more information or skills, if they choose to spend their time wisely.

32.

DO IT TODAY

It's mantra time: Do It Today (DIT). There's a Biblical truth here. Tomorrow will have its own, new, problems. Beat the deadlines. Expect that each deadline will be beaten and that your requests, orders and instructions will be carried out, with sweet fragrance, before the day is through. That means when the last person – and that should be you – packs up to head home.

If DIT becomes iffy, hand over the task to someone else, as I have explained in Chapter 30. Divide the tasks in today-deliverables. Frequent feedback is more efficient than the "Oh, No!" resulting from a task misaligned when completed.

Understand the enormous difference between to **delegate** and to **abdicate**. Delegation requires a set time and a mechanism for feedback, evaluation and correction. All else is grenade-throwing abdication, which is easy and is obviously also destructive. DIT fits nicely with delegation, with a set feedback and reporting mechanism.

Delegation requires your involvement and, where possible, a light touch of mentoring, or whatever you call it when wisdom and direction are imparted in a non-threatening way. With delegation, you are part of the feedback process. It will do your blood pressure a world of good to wander down and see the troops and find out how they are doing, and what they are doing to get to the **what**. Giving tasks without also requiring feedback is like feeding fish without then catching them. Stock up your larder.

33.

THE FIRST RULE OF MOTIVATION: WHAT'S IN IT FOR ME?

If you put your hand up, fingers splayed, each finger can be a countdown on What's In It For Me? (WIIFM?) Incentives can and should motivate. If the person you are trying to 'motivate' has no personal motto, it will be difficult to spur him on. In order to "keep your job" is a trite objective. It's also a highly effective WIIFM? In fact, fear motivates thrice as much as reward. The Heat is more effective than the Light, in the short term. Ultimately, the intrinsic value of doing things should become its own reward, as it was for the kids we used to be and it often still is for our own kids.

Then there is the turbo of incentives. Like moving to turbo power, there is a lag, and then a price to pay afterwards. When the incentive has lapsed, the winners of the Boat Cruise announced, the output level is hardly going to remain at 100% of what it was before the competition. Of course, the question on everyone's lips will be: "What is next year's prize?"

Thus the trap of enslavement to the kicker is dug by the well-meaning management team themselves. The moment we ritualise this, whether in politics or in business, an extended expectation is created. It magically morphs into an entitlement that can only be dislodged with dynamite and tears.

Where does the sweet spot of motivation lie? In the individual carrot, or in the corporate buffet? In the unreachable, or mundane? What should the refresher rate be? Annual update, or constant change?

Isn't it refreshing to be confronted by the art of motivation where science falls into a stupor? Here's some guidance on my approach to motivation:

Ask. The expectations of people are more modest and mundane when solicited by someone whom they suspect may view them as greedy and self-serving. Not that you would ever do that! Modesty is a virtue for most. Ask, prod, perhaps. Getting someone to set their own high bar can be a strong motivator.

Be fair. Every child knows what's fair without being taught. Fairness should be company-wide, not just applicable to the sales force. Bonuses should be company-wide, not just for the collections department. Fair rewards are cornerstones of motivation.

Its status must exceed the reward itself. The cash will be spent, the trip long-gone, but if you play it right the accolades will reverberate in the memory and on the CV. The standing ovation doesn't pay more bills, but when you add it to the monetary side, it can do magic to the willpower.

Be personal. It's your attention that is craved, actually that of your position, not of your tanned hide in a garage-wide smile, with stunning dental work for all to see. Let the winner feel: "Power hath anointed me; I am special!" Go give your time in eyeball dollars. It is worth millions.

Good luck. It is difficult, but do not neglect your troops' sense of play and adventure.

34.

THE PAIN OF TAKING SOMETHING AWAY IS THREE TIMES STRONGER THAN THE JOY YOU CREATED WHEN YOU GAVE IT OUT

True. It is fun to give but much worse to lose something you have already received. We are an acquisitive species. Just look at ladies' shoe collections – perhaps as a throwback of our reptilian brain that begs for more of everything. Then the mammalian brain selects the good from the bad. Except for women choosing shoes, or for men choosing fishing rods or other boy-toys!

The application of giving with emotion and expectation seems to reflect our higher selves. This is good, except when things are then taken away. Apparently the personality reverts to its crocodile brain.

Be careful what you promise. Be judicious when you give and fair when you threaten to, or actually do, reverse the privileges and rewards. Restoring them will secure one-third joy only, sadly. Ask any politician. This 3x rule should guide you to make modest promises, never to be broken.

In general, life is a game of never-ending hope. Our final hope is extinguished on the deathbed. Except that another fervent one trades this fading life for a possible better one in Heaven, through reincarnation, or in hope of Valhalla.

Play the game of hope carefully. Over-indulgence will breed spoilt brats, but behaving like a boarding-school master at home and in the office will attract scorn and pranks. Being a father figure is the easiest path, as long as you first draw the boundaries and then encourage youthful exuberance. Cast yourself in the mould where maturity is fostered instead of childishness being constrained.

35.

NEVER ACCEPT: "I THINK". ONLY: "I KNOW". NEVER: "I DON'T KNOW." ALWAYS: "I'LL FIND OUT"

I guess the IBM mantra of **think** got lost in translation after 40 years. Instead of exhorting the deeper pondering of the not-yet-known, it has become an opt-out from facts. It is unacceptable and downright dangerous to answer a pertinent question with: "I think …" It not only shows sloppy opinionating, but also a tenuous grasp of facts and realities and it is a dangerous trap. Do we have enough cash? "I think so." Should we double the marketing spend? Terminate the contract in Brazil? "I think so."

This is not a statement of assent; it is an unsubstantiated guess that is placing the skids under a moving leviathan, and to everybody's detriment. It seems that people resent being caught out when they don't know the answer, and then cloak their temporary ignorance in a guestimate that can unleash a horror. Stop this practice in its tracks. Forever.

Each question needs to be answered with facts. There is no shame in saying: "I'll find out …" and then coming back with a researched and verified answer. Never accept a guess, unless you ask for an *opinion*, and then treat it as such.

Few of us have all the facts at hand. I would urge you to build a daily dashboard where everyone can see the things that should be measured, and their quantum. When you ask for additional facts outside of this, it should obviously trigger the inclusion of that answer in the Daily Executive Summary on the dashboard. Or at least force the repository of that answer in a place where it is accessible at a moment's notice.

I often make fun of my under-30s, who proclaim that Google is their friend. Ask any question and an answer is search engine-produced in short shrift. Sometimes the web surfers lack the breadth of insight to choose between various versions of facts and opinions. What stymies me is when I later ask the exact question and see a rush back to the net. The answers do not seem to stick when the memory is in the cloud.

36.

THERE ARE TWO TYPES OF MISTAKE

Easy and cheap to fix, or expensive and difficult to fix?

As with my 'leak a little money' idea to encourage innovation, you must get your people to fail a little, ever so often. Help them set some avenue that's good for the enterprise and it'll be great if they can achieve it. Show, tell, and then stand back. Lend a hand when the going gets rough.

Without sufficient safe practice, how else will they learn how to walk, run, sprint, and move rapidly and efficiently in *parkour* mode when needed? Don't run out of ideas. Don't limit their ideas to their specialities either, with the one *proviso*: do make any failure of theirs cheap to fix.

There is progress in a fixed fall-down and get-up. Staying down is a defeat and must be punished by dismissal. Do get them on the cheap ponies before saddling up the thoroughbreds. Or else there could be tears all round, with a lot of yours, too.

Think through the consequences carefully. Then look for bright eyes and stand back. The wanna-do potential will shape your thoughts about the next round of promotions.

Deadwood is not restricted to the over 60s or under 25s. It could just be more prevalent there. To get the butterflies dancing and the fingers itching, set seemingly insoluble tasks with small, winning increments. Have the patch and solution handy for blowouts and be the first to offer encouragement when the path seems more thistle than laurel. After all, you're the one they want to please.

37.

NEVER DO SOMETHING FOR SOMEONE THAT THEY ARE CAPABLE OF DOING FOR THEMSELVES

Make this the first lesson of your life-long mentoring, at all levels. Ken Blanchard simplified the show-tell-watch-delegate mechanism eloquently in *The One Minute Manager*, but there is a catch.

The delegated tasks and responsibilities will often run into new territory and not everyone's risk profile allows them to hopscotch though minefields with abandon. They may try and retreat, ask and repeat, but at some stage the buck will land back on your desk.

Hence this advice. It is easy to accept an upwardly-delegated task, as you yourself can probably do it unconsciously, competently and in a flash.

Resist the urge to show-off as the delegator. Never limit what you think the *delegatee* is capable of, even if the job needs a fair bit of additional input. Your *minions* want to become *maxions*. They need to be pushed to achieve, not just left to produce.

Delegating tough stuff, and often out-of-comfort-zone responsibilities, is your specific domain and an art forever being fine-tuned.

Push someone a little to gauge his level of discomfort. A response with fear and anxiety will mean he is at the limits of his comfort, while anger and disgust mean he is being under-deployed.

Here's a guide: everyone has defined levels of self-worth. These can change and improve, and they are often directly linked to their current rank, not to their capability.

If the task is above the level of comfort of someone, it may trigger an above-comfort reaction. Thus the level of fear about giving a speech or a presentation depends on the person who is presented with this task and on his level of confidence. This can be remedied, and you probably know a number of ways to ease him into that capability and to get a blossoming ego in return. All for the better.

At the other end of the scale, a demeaning task that is below someone's self-worth will trigger annoyance, or worse. Anyone can wash a car, but asking a manager to wash your flashy wheels may be seen as demeaning to his position, and rightly so. This cannot be remedied. It is plain wrong.

Watch the level of your instruction in relation to the position and the persona of the unlucky underling being tasked with something unexpected. Watch the boomerang as well. Never do for them what they are capable of doing themselves, especially when there is a cry for help. Remember to skip the level where you show them how it's done. Tell. Watch. Delegate. That is your answer.

38.

SAYING NO RAISES THE QUALITY OF THE ARGUMENT

"No" is not a showstopper. It is a request for better, more relevant and valuable persuasion. It is a commonly-held belief, learned from childhood, that a firm tone of voice is the end of the conversation. Oh, no.

You failed in *that* argument. Obviously you have failed to convince your protagonist, your customer or the gentle person on the other side of the cocktail.

Now is the time to raise the level of the argument, piling on more facts and a better angle, all towards a better understanding.

"No" can be a fantastic tool. It can get to the real reasons why a request has landed on the table. Use it to mean: "Tell me more and then I'll get better at it." This two-letter monosyllable should be interpreted as asking just this question.

If you are convinced of your argument, confidence and sincerity will win the day. Raising the level of the argument is just a prolonged way of sifting time. If you give up early, you don't really want to win it. Keep at it with conviction and raise the stakes in every round.

Expect your hand-wringers to seek exceptions, changes and favours. Make them raise the argument to a place where they are also convinced that they must either make sense or accept that they have an unsound idea. Don't just stonewall it from your side. Let them learn.

39.

IF YOU CANNOT GET TO THE ANSWER, ESCALATE THE PROBLEM

When the workday ends, we expect all tasks to be completed, as tomorrow will bring its own set of challenges.

A guideline that may serve you well is to un-brood the issues. If something cannot be solved, it must be escalated early – bearing in mind the rule that when it reaches the next level up, the recipient won't carry out the task himself, but will only help the junior who is stuck to find the answer.

The escalation elevator must go to the top, hopefully one level at a time. Sometimes a minor delegation ambushes me, with the expectation of the *deus ex machina* of the CEO's magic touch. Tragically, I am fallible and so are you. More often my inspiration and guidance is wanted and needed, not my witty and pointed solution.

There is some ego involved and you would be well advised to get rid of the culture of: "I can't do it!" If it cannot be solved, escalate it.

Escalation should become a habit, as it fosters learning. Can't get a recalcitrant debtor on the phone? Call his boss. Then the boss's boss. Then get your CEO to call his CEO, or to drop him a friendly line, requesting someone down there to call your anxious department.

It is not only interactions that should be escalated. Frustrations should be, too. PC slow? Scratchy phone line? Damp washroom? All these are the classic demotivating 'hygiene factors' that impede performance if left unsolved.

Is there a perfect workplace? Yours might be exactly that for some people. Others march to the beat of the free lunch, an air-conditioned parking spot, which you may not be able or willing to provide. There are hordes of little time nibblers that constrain staff. Make it a project to find them and eliminate them. Open the channels if these persist. You may not be able to solve everything, but, hey, that's where delegation comes in. It's reverse escalation!

40.

WHAT IS EVERY POSITION'S PRIMARY, MEASURABLE, ONE-SENTENCE OBJECTIVE?

How does each person in your organisation know when they are successful?

In the ISO 9001 templates, every position is well described and every task is mapped in terms of best practises.

Yet it is imperative that a single sentence should be the guide to success, the one-liner that defines the measure that everyone should know and that all should abide by. Make sure they understand, believe and live it.

One of your primary roles is to give structure. This structure must lead to a meaningful existence.

Our receptionist's key role is defined as follows: to be the shortest route between a customer's problem and an answer. This is Joyce's world. Now her position description echoes her primary, measurable, objective (PMO), – just what she is expected to do above all. It's not just handling the switchboard and putting through calls as needed. There is a **why** built in. Often she can help, guide, and dramatically enhance the company's reputation. She is magic. She saves time, frustration and effort for the customer who is calling in, as well us for the person who will be fielding the call. Joyce will diagnose who is on the line, and why. So calling in won't lead to the same questions being asked each time the caller is re-directed from one (wrong) person to another, until he stumbles upon someone to help. There is a solution on the way from the first: "Hello".

Joyce at reception knows as much as possible about the company. How else will she know how to help? If every position in the organisation has a PMO, each can be evaluated objectively. Evaluations are still on the ISO template, but beside the achievements that each employee lists, he is evaluated on his ability and consistency in doing the one thing that is his focus.

Every position should be so defined. What would yours be as the CEO? What's your PMO? If all positions, then, are measurable, shouldn't all positions participate in the bonus scheme?

41.

UN-DRUDGE ALL TASKS. YOU ARE PAYING YOUR CHAMPIONS TO THINK AND IMPROVE, NOT TO REPEAT MENIAL ACTIONS

Automate! Undo! Simplify! Don't complicate! Your people must leave the office energised for their *real* life. If not, you are failing them.

We want to prosper, not exist. We need to be fruitful, not busy. There's a horde of such one-liners in the ether, all for a good reason. Do you drive slaves, or are you in the business of getting ahead?

Another line: at five o'clock your assets go home. Their *real* lives start when they park in the drive at home. They have three or four hours of a home-life that must reinforce why they want to come back as early as possible tomorrow.

Their motivation for coming back the next day won't be eight hours of drudgery, meaningless tasks, the repetition of inane actions, or wasting their time on something that keeps them looking busy.

I want to fire anyone who looks like they are working too hard. I would first have a heart-to-heart in the mirror to practice talking to that guy to test the assumption that I have un-drudged those tasks. Then I would need a very good reason to keep the finger off the trigger. Somehow something became over-urgent and some system failed to expedite it before the deadline.

I am hooked on using Excel and yet I cannot understand accountants who need to export the financials into Excel for massaging, checking, report writing and all the bean polishing, before all is dished up with a nice béchamel sauce and fresh cherries. What's going on here? This is being busy.

Ditto about anyone with a pen in their hand. Just what notes are you creating outside of the official reports, or the note section in the customer profiles?

To un-drudge, you should automate as much as possible. Get a security guard at the printer, too. Just why is that page not in a PDF, and ready to send, share, save, or file? Have a relentless methodology for weeding out the deadly, bad habits that suck up work-time and clog the day.

I need my troops to drink the best coffee in town, sit around the large, domed, open-area in the middle of the office ground floor, and share ideas. There are no doors, nor walls and thus no offices. Only the boardrooms are enclosed. Anyone with a pile of paper arouses suspicion. Anyone leaving for home with what looks like a file is a candidate for the high jump.

What is the drudge? Ask and you will be told. What wastes time? Prepare the shears. What do your chaps *want* to do? Be prepared to be amazed. They do know.

42.

Any change will create tension like stretching a rubber band

To relieve the tension, one or both of the sides must move towards the other. Or else the tension will remain.

Which side will move? Which side should move? Remember you are probably on side B, doing the pulling.

How far to pull? The further from the resting state, the higher the tension.

In general we dislike tension, change and upheaval. In medieval times we feared The Stranger, and newcomers to the village needed a letter of introduction, had to report to the chief constable and to keep their whereabouts updated there.

Pestilence, robbers and sociopaths were all successfully kept at bay by our ancestors, or else we wouldn't be here today.

The scepticism of, and resistance to, change is deep rooted and well founded. You thought you had cloaked yourself in the magician's robes, but you appear to have stepped off your broom in full sight of those aghast at your coming.

Change is not fun, as Niccolò Machiavelli noted:

> *"It must be remembered that there is nothing more difficult to plan, more doubtful of success, nor more dangerous to manage than a new system. For the initiator has the enmity of all who would profit by the preservation of the old institution and merely lukewarm defenders in those who gain by the new ones."*

Success is not assured. Benefits are not certain. If you are convinced, then do like Cortez: burn your boats. You had better have a plan B at the ready. Be prepared to lead the breach of the ramparts and risk your reputation irrevocably. Stretch the tension properly and keep at it until your Luddites come around.

The resistors? Again quoting from Machiavelli's *The Prince*:

> *"A man who is used to acting in one way never changes;*
> *he must come to ruin when the times, in changing, no*
> *longer are in harmony with his ways."*

Of course you understand Darwinism (more on this later). Machiavelli also wrote:

> *"People should either be caressed or crushed. If you do*
> *them minor damage they will get their revenge; but if*
> *you cripple them there is nothing they can do. If you*
> *need to injure someone, do it in such a way that you do*
> *not have to fear their vengeance."*

Read your Machiavelli. His advice has withstood 400 years. Be tough, then nice. NOT nice, then tough.

43.

YOUR CHAMPIONS MUST FIT IN AND PERFORM

Develop your halfway-there warriors to both fit in and perform, or send them off the field. Jack Welsh popularised the matrix that defined the best ones as fitting the corporate ethos and performing to the corporate standard. In arguing that your champions must both fit in and perform, I mean that if they meet just one of these requirements, you will have a half-disaster in the making. If they meet neither, that means a full-blown one.

Life can be a little trickier than that. The gradients in either measurement complicate this. The true champion combines high focus with high energy. Having no focus means energetic isometrics (getting tired, but going nowhere); having no energy means potential effort (all ready, but no go).

Many of your elites vacillate between the targets. They're human after all, unlike you – the emotionally controlled, stainless steel, egocentric demigod in their midst.

How do you charge them up? That's a real chore, Mr Missile Launcher. You need to fuel them up, point them well and let them fly. This is a daily job: watching for the signs of a flagging spirit and a flaccid approach. As in golf, they have played perfect shots from many angles, but how can one play a beauty every time a club swings?

Too often their interpretation of what you say is not in line with your intended message. Their elevator speech of what each is doing is off-colour, off-the-cuff and inconsistent. The message must be clear, repeatable and it must ring true.

Through repetition, the message should become second nature. Inherently, little can go wrong if a missile's course is set up properly. You must get the best out of your launches. Check and double check against your people firing off at half-cock.

44.

LICENCE YOUR TIGERS FOR THEIR TASKS

Can they type 45 words per minute. If not, why did you hand them a PC?

Can they operate Advanced Excel? Only then give them access to the spreadsheets.

Train them, test them, licence them and reward them. On a continuous basis. Your infantry is giving up their best, most valuable time five-days-a-week, when they could be doing real-life stuff. Use their time really, really well. They may resemble wage slaves, but they are your biggest link to success.

They trade in their real worth for security. You are paying them less than they would be worth if they were running their own business; this gap is where your profits come from.

What are the other things you expect them to do as if they intuitively know it all? Should they master the Accounting system to Advanced Level? Should you make Certified Project Management a requirement for everyone scheduling tasks and jobs? Even a *VoIP for Dummies* book gifted to your telecoms decision-makers would put them ahead of your competition.

Make the minimum levels of competence part of the job requirement. A good typing speed is a massive advantage, and typing accuracy is an even bigger advantage. Sadly, we've found no other enterprise that sees things in this way. You should implement and enforce this in yours.

All our PC drivers get to do Excel to Advanced stage. All have iPads with a minimum number of apps. Everyone has been trained on MindMapping and iThoughts is the programme of choice. Increasing everyone's levels of excellence and competence pays serious dividends and boosts confidence all round. We test typing speed every three months and this test is mandatory. If you expect the best from your dragon-tamers, equip them well.

45.

LABOURER *VS* GARDENER

On Saturday mornings I get to see my euphemistically-named land-scape engineer. We don't cross paths during weekdays, as he nor-mally leaves long before I am able to escape the office.

I expect him to be a proper gardener, telling me what I need to do to make his efforts successful and to improve the status of the garden. The fuel for the lawnmower won't last another week. The shears should be taken for a service as autumn is coming up. The pH near the swan pond is too high, so should we order lime before planting the nasturtiums? With his feedback, we plan the week. He shows me the results from the previous week and awaits my com-ments. We discuss things that could be done, and he guides me on what's possible, what's feasible and what's necessary. I want a pretty garden for the family to enjoy and relax in. He delivers that. He's a proper gardener.

What I don't want is a labourer. That's the guy who must ask me what he must do each day. One who tells me on a Saturday that the lawnmower has been broken since Tuesday. He couldn't plant the nasturtiums because of … whatever reason. There is blame and a culture of no shame for missed tasks and deadlines.

Similarly, the workers in your enterprise are divided between the responsibly proactive and the living dead. Like yeast, an economic principle may spread. It's called: 'The tragedy of the commons.' Why should some do their utmost, while others who focus only on their own narrow interests can get away with less?

Test for those that are the gardeners. Cull, prune and fertilise amongst the workforce accordingly.

You can change what people know. You cannot always change what they do, or how they approach their work.

46.

DOES EVERY POSITION IN YOUR FIRM HAVE A BACKUP, A PLAN B?

This should be in the form of a set of procedures *and* must contain details of another person who is equipped to take the baton in case of absence.

This is the lesson we had all waxed and sorted before we got bigger and into a different league. People take vacation, need unplanned sick days and move on, up, or out.

It helps to know exactly what all of your people do, how they do it and where they do it, from the files and ledgers to the quote folder and other details.

Not only does it help the stand-ins to cope, but you will realise how imperative it is that these tasks are described, and that the interactions are all documented.

With a "See you later" to the departing one, the plan B person can take on the caretaker role. Of course you have had a dry run here, too, to avoid any nasty surprises.

Plan B and person B must be debriefed and assessed after the absence, as well. What could be improved? What went wrong? What other evil that was previously unforeseen is bubbling under? Getting this firmly in hand gets you way over halfway to ISO certification, too.

Turn to your systems, too. Plan B, and sometimes plan C, becomes desirable. Is there a backup plan for your external support? Losing an Audit Manager or a supplier would require quick-thinking. Better to do this at leisure, beforehand. Never run out of good plans.

47.

THE COURT JESTER CAN TELL THE KING THE TRUTH

You should offer reward when the truth is spoken to power, however galling, humbling, or inconvenient this refreshing and necessary action might be. All too often a commitment to speaking the truth is mere lip service. Hardly a single whistle-blower is ever honoured. The Jester could once tell the truth without fear of personal consequences, but that was then and this is now.

Does morality clash with business sense? If it does, reconsider why you find yourself in this predicament. Life is short, friends are few, but regret is everlasting. Make sure that your voice is one of reason, of honesty, and that you are the shining light on the hill. Would you really sell your soul and reputation for a marginal call? Think!

It often seems that business advantages are explored closer to the quicksand than most would be comfortable with. The true extent of the criminal empires spanning the earth may not be known, but their successors are lurking in the corridors of respectability, mindgaming their entry into a world of no accountability.

Listen to your Jesters. Never go *ad hominem*. The messenger might well be just the bravest of an entire division, where *all* of them think your latest stunt stinks. You must be beyond reproach. While it's not great coming second to the bastard who flouted the rules, tomorrow is another day. Then you will measure your actions against your beliefs, and your way against the universe that chose you as the lucky one that you are. Don't disappoint.

Be fair, always. Fairness is the one thing you cannot explain away from any child. Unfairness hurts, from very early on. The notion may have been numbed over years of school bullying and other miscreantic behaviour by your predecessor.

So let peace reign and Joe the Fair take the throne amidst a new era of hope and joy. With his honest and unafraid Italian pantomime troupe of Pierrot, Columbine and the others.

48.

WORK TOWARDS GRADUATION

Your own children need to grow up, to learn more, achieve and to graduate. That's your hope, anyway. You must offer the same path, with a gradient, to your people, too.

When someone feels they have better prospects outside our tribe, we hold a Graduation Party. We tell everyone to where, and to what, the departing one is graduating. We were unable to match such a position. We are also extremely and genuinely happy that there is a graduation. *Bon voyage* and well-wishes are said, too, and a farewell gift is offered.

Graduation prospects arise through the acquisition of additional knowledge, sometimes called qualifications, and the confidence of achievement, which compel the hunter within to find new hunting grounds, where the trophies are bigger and more plentiful.

You need to encourage this. Not everyone leaves. A few do, and sometimes they are the people you genuinely want to stay. In the process you are increasing the capacity for better output, better decisions and all the good things that improvement brings. Everyone should have a plan to adding skills and responsibilities to those skills already bedded down, and the opportunities to show just what they're worth.

Your own graduation is imminent. The average CEO's cycle between "Help us!" and "Pack your bags!" is rather short, probably three to five years, or so. That's the limit of your fresh approach and of your results becoming humdrum or stale in a world that is ever-changing. Then comes the fresh demand of miracles from the same players, via a new coach.

Your skills need to be honed. Your reaction time, insight, wisdom and ability to make a ragtag squad into a *Wehrmacht*, need to be upgraded constantly.

The very skills that got you to be the CEO are often not the skills that you need to keep you there, so improve your repertoire.

In time you will face the question, temptation or inevitability: your own graduation from formal employment to become the lauded entrepreneur or investor.

Many have walked that plank, but few have succeeded. Internationally, it is informally known as the 5% Club. That's the success rate after five years of all start-up businesses. It's an appalling success rate.

The 'free man' is described by Nassim Taleb in *Antifragile* as one who can fix the problems and understand the business and not only via delegation and control. He contrasts this with the two other types: slaves and slave drivers. Many would-be or dabbling entrepreneurs from the C-Suite reckon themselves as 'The Man', but mostly they are slave drivers with money. Their investments are usually lousy, their efforts puerile in comparison to their former performance. It probably takes five years to make the transition from 'Corporate Slave Driver' to a successful 'Free Man'.

It is a hard, hard school, with few shortcuts. Like swimming, it cannot be learned from a book. As a wealthy, successful, retired or fired CEO you are at a massive disadvantage. Your ego does not easily lend itself to learning the lessons from the ground up. In the immortal words of the Marquess of Halifax:

> "A prince who will not undergo the Difficulty of Understanding must undergo the Danger of Trusting."

Decide if a seriously long period of understanding is what you have in mind, or else get a hobby and focus on your publicly-traded investments.

49.

OUTGROWING YOUR FIRST STAFF

Here's an oft-ignored and sad reality. The staff you started off with may no longer fit the bill. Those who trusted and supported your spindly-legged ventures, or who boosted your meteoric ascent to the egosphere, have earned your eternal gratitude. They don't necessarily belong on the inside track to follow the future trajectory.

The time may come when different or – and this is painful! – a superior set of skills are needed to step on the gas. Those familiar eyes, which knew you from garage start-up days and mopped up after your previous disasters, will not always understand or forgive your present patent cruelty and inhuman ingratitude in the promotion game.

Here's some guidance, and it comes with my heartfelt sympathy:
1. Bring in some A-team players to lift everyone else's output
If you need to promote over the head of incumbents, go outside of the company. Get the best candidate. Anyone promoted from the inside will be a latecomer and you don't want to have to adjudicate that standoff. Get star quality and it will justify itself. A bigger company gives access to, and can afford, better middle management. So aim to get there. Soon.

2. Builders vs bureaucrats
You need to make this clear company-wide. There are stages in the enterprise's life cycle where it needs different types of management. The old Greiner model defines five stages of a company's growth and crises in its life cycle. Structure the enterprise in a different way and set some distance between yourself and the old-faithful. Make sure that you are seen hamming it up with the un-promoted. Regu-

larly. There is still a bond from way back and they will have at least the bragging rights that the top dog couldn't have got this far without them.

50.

YOUR PERSONAL MANAGEMENT STYLE

What's your personal style? If you don't know, ask your PA. Prepare to be deflated by the response, so work on developing the persona of the Commander-In-Chief, who exudes confidence and trust. Never ever give up on this.

My style is "无为而无不为"
"*Wi wei er wu bu wei.*" Do nothing, but nothing is left undone.

The Chinese description is best explained in a poem:

> "*The Sage is occupied with the unspoken*
> *and acts without effort.*
> *Teaching without verbosity,*
> *producing without possessing,*
> *creating without regard to result,*
> *claiming nothing,*
> *the Sage has nothing to lose.*"

To me this equates to accomplishment without effort; making everything look so easy.

This is my 'way' to inspire and lead. Decisions and actions appear to flow without effort. I conceal disappointments and fix errors, so only the good results are visible. This defines me.

Find your style and develop it. There are many pairs of eyes looking up, with their gaze fixed on you, searching for a mentor and someone to hold up as example to their kids. Become that person.

51.

CONTROL FEAR AND ANXIETY, AND ANGER

Under severe stress, your IQ rolls back to that of an ape. Perhaps your IQ is rather sensitive and needs little coaxing to round the arms and scrape the knuckles. The count-to-ten is an old but tried strategy to keep you from the inevitable Grand Jury hearing you might foist on yourself through uncontrolled emotion and actions. Perhaps there will be talk of the straightjacket, too.

Cortisol, the stress hormone, is your enemy and the 'macho' hormone testosterone is your ally. Holding your body in power poses can bring down the pressure and enable you to regain your cool and lower stress. I would advise you to get yourself out of yourself in a stressful situation by securing a good grip on yourself and on your hormones. Stand. Pose. Think. Lower your voice. Start asking questions. Until your blood pressure and blood sugar are back to normal and the testo is back in control.

You dislike surprises and everyone knows this by now. The chance of a confrontation is lessened, and the bad news will be filtered in absorbable batches.

Your first impulse is toward action. Hannibal would have had you for breakfast. It was only the withdrawal of Scipio and the luring of elephant man to battle, on his own terms, which saved Rome. This is your duty: get real, corroborated info before you let out the battle cry. This may seem like inaction, but it is not. It is regaining control of the situation. You need to fight battles on your *own* turf as far as possible.

Time might be of the essence. Sometimes you need to act calmly, and delay is called for. Your largest customer just defected? Send the peace offering wrapped around the 24-month penalty clause you negotiated when the fresh bloom of beauty was on the cheeks of the relationship.

Anxiety is even worse. Anxiety shows up in uncontrolled no-contingency, monsters that lurk in your corridors. Go back to the risk list and revisit the effects, the alternatives and the ease of implementation. Background anxiety will fritter away your confidence and your health. It is contagious, Superman. You do not want those green kryptonite rocks close to you. Get rid of the worry attitude. After all, you don't *get* ulcers. You *give* them.

52.

BE LIKE NYLON

Fortitude is glorified in the Calvin Coolidge speech: 'Press on in hand'. These thoughts on hardship by my old nemesis, attorney Mr Muyburgh, have stood the test of time and describe resilience even better:

> *"Don't be strong as steel. Steel is hard and inflexible and cold. It bends a little and if bent a lot, it will crack and break.*
>
> *Being as strong as steel is not good enough. Be as strong as nylon. You can bend nylon. Nylon bends and bends some more. It keeps bending. It never breaks. Be like nylon, endlessly bending and springing back."*

Too often we encounter competition from other firms which are willing to sail a little too close to the wind, pushing a little harder than necessary to get an advantage, by scuffing against the limits of the law and good practice, thinking that the law is cast in nylon, too. It is not.

Compromise is sometimes necessary for the practicalities of governance. It must be unthinkable where your principles are concerned. Don't go there.

Do not cultivate the habit of peering over the line between right and wrong, even if it is just to smell the odour of the other side. You are above reproach. Your leaning will be the go-to sign to rush over the top for everyone in your team who has been awaiting your implied approval. Resist the push. When pushed there, spring back like nylon, too.

53.

CONFIDENCE DRIVES ALMOST EVERYTHING

As a kid you heard it, tried it and maybe even mastered, the art of sounding confident and plausible. You may have tried it to pick up girls. Sometime you might have got it right, circumstances allowing. Sometimes a more confident kid snatched her away. So what did *he* have that you didn't, and why does it matter?

It's still all about confidence – yours and hers. Or theirs, if you want to extend the analogy to the enterprise. Your team will generally do what you want them to if you can show them a winning way, one in which you confidently believe.

Doing things well instils confidence, the level of confidence drives the level of dominance, and thus the pecking order follows. Thanks to which you're the #1 in your industry and perhaps so at home, too.

Confidence is an emotional projection that shapes the expectations of the other person. "Trust me; I know what I'm doing." That got you the first kiss, and the last laugh, too. It's ongoing and it is the one thing you must cultivate, and absolutely fake if you need to.

Your troops aren't keen on abandoning ship, but if they detect a fall in your self-esteem this will have them jumping over the ramparts and into the arms of the opposition. In a flash. If you falter, go watch some YouTube of Apollo Robbins and Pamela Meyer on TED, or episodes in the *Lie to Me* series to get some guidance on how to fake the very short interval before your demise.

How to build confidence? Validate the other person in the first sentence. Create punching space for yourself. Don't set yourself up as The Answer to Any Question right there and then. Hear them out. Ask around. Get opinions. Let your answer simmer. Be in charge. Trot out the beauty, to their astonishment. Remember also the comment of former New York Mayor, Fiorello LaGuardia: "I don't make many mistakes, but when I do it's a beaut!"

The obverse side is your ego. While confidence will boost it, keep it reined in and tethered. Your world is not a competition until you step up against the sort of competition with whom your people will not easily do battle. Your victories there will be hollow and self-destructive. Go play golf. It's humbling. If that doesn't work, try long-distance swimming for a worthwhile battle against your inner self. I have, and it works. Confidence? Yes. Egotism? No.

54.

THERE ARE TWO WAYS OF GOING NEW BUSINESS

Here is a timeless phrase about evaluating business opportunities: "Either you bring the experience and leave with the cash. Or you bring the cash and leave with the experience."

Let's expand a bit on the ignorance theme. The history of mergers and acquisitions is littered with debris piled so high that it is unfathomable that such value-destruction is still allowed, and not banned from the universe.

Let's assume that egos are not at play. Although it's likely they account for a fair portion of what is going on here. After all, size does matter for most men, so the Short Man syndrome is pervasive, too. Many underperforming CEOs distract attention from a lack of organic growth through the excitement of size – by purchasing market share.

Let's also assume that the target entity is known, that all the incompatibles are past the ironing board stage, that the holes are plugged and that mysterious quality of a good fit is creating a dense cloud of pheromones in the boardroom.

It's decision time. This will, of course, lead to consequences. Both intended ones, and that old foe of the ego: Murphy's Law of Unintended Consequences.

The extent of your experience will determine your degree of success. Like your first attempt at getting a girlfriend, these things take a bit of time and practice to generate wisdom. New business? New product line expansion? Expanding abroad?

All these are subject to what I call "Geffen's Law of the Two Ways", named after the wizened, stone-hearted and bloodless woman I served in my first CEO position as a tender 29-year-old.

First do your homework. Do it well, or you may pay school fees. Either you bring the experience and reap rewards, or you suffer the humiliation of the novice. Learning expensive lessons through those many 'mistakes' you will subsequently want to label as 'experience'.

55.

IF THE CEO IS NOT OUT SPENDING 20% OF HIS TIME IN FRONT OF CUSTOMERS, HE IS OUT OF TOUCH

Business and management writer, Tom Peters, promoted the notion of spending one day each week in your market with your customers. That was in the 1980s, before the internet. Today there are myriad ways to keep in touch with your customers and you can suck info from the web at a rate that can be overwhelming.

All this is preparation for the grand show: the CEO on parade. There is no better morale-booster than your own presence in front of a new prospect. You are the Lucky Token, the Magic Touch. As long as you sit there, smiling and nodding and radiating wisdom, your people will be showing off for your benefit. Have you ever noticed the jump in the hit rate when you're around? It's astonishing how much it increases if you are ever out there, in front of your customers and prospective catches, which is where you should be. Oh, it's so easy to hide behind your big mahogany desk; you being so important and all that.

"Aquila muscas non capit," said Julius the Caesar. "An eagle doesn't catch flies." You might think it's not worth your while? Where else can you make the most impact, now that your den is well organised and the management is empowered to make decisions and face consequences? They love you when you're out of the office. At last they get to do something worthwhile, when your beady eyes are elsewhere.

How much time, collectively, is your entire organisation spending in front of your customers? 50%? 10%? 1%? Is it the belief, then, that the rest of the time should be spent keeping the organisation together?

If the Debtor Department isn't still spending 50% of its time in front of customers, the people working there are not building relationships. If Sales are not spending 80% of their time in front of customers, it may mean they are running scared.

The excuse they will often give you is that there's always a wailing call in an unread e-mail and a grinding necessity of paperwork, and so on. Or is there, really? Should there be? It would be best for you to get a pool of corporate vehicles and start scheduling mandatory time for the team outside the comfort of watching TV, oops, I mean a PC screen. Start them spending productive time in the hunting grounds.

56.

APPLY THE 80/20 RULE RELENTLESSLY

Pareto Analysis, which is a method for choosing the most important changes to make, is not a new concept. It is widely ignored, even though it is a very relevant measurement. You have limited time and unlimited opportunities. How does one choose well?

Start with your resources. Are your people spending time in Pareto? Reverse the question. What takes up 80% of their time? Eliminate this and the rest will expand. Is it easy? This is why the elbows are freed for better manoeuvrability. With more resources available, you may start pursuing the way forward.

Many describe such moves as strategy, but perhaps it is just sound business. As with farming, you have to live by Darwin and keep trying for a better way forward.

The best way is to improve the way things are done. Repackage things in simpler and more usable formats for your customers, and innovate by adding incrementally to what you can offer. The history of commerce is littered with fantastical disasters, with people stretching too far beyond the basics which they could properly grasp.

Not everyone can run Apple Corp. Only a few can understand the single-minded concept of selling third-party items that will only work on their own devices. It was never about Jonny Ives' brilliant execution of Steve's hardware ideas, but an iTunes and App store that rolls in the billions, with the buyers always spending more and more on hardware.

Microsoft hasn't had ground-breaking ideas since launching Office in 1990. It has tried relentlessly to reinvent itself. The original, since improved, juggernaut may keep driving it forward for a decade or more. What then?

Pareto again. Where's the margin? Where's the growth? On which product lines? It is wishful thinking and time-wasting to push hard in a direction that is not profitable. Stay on course and treasure your 80% margin contributors, your sales guys bringing in 80%, the industry where 80% of your sales comes from, the regions that generate 80%, and so on. Analyse. Understand. Learn and focus on every possible Pareto and then make Pareto-inspired investment decisions.

57.

Believing in something good might mean that you are blinded to something even better

Let's call this the Fallacy of Perfection. If it works, don't screw with it. Or something to that effect. There *are* some things that are perfect. Mom's apple crumble and the goodnight kiss from your firstborn. However, most business ideas and processes can be improved on. And drastically, too.

Let's assume you are able to develop a mindset that is critical of everything around you and you crave to understand both the width and depth of the subjects that affect you. As a decidedly average open-water swimmer, with my age counting against me, I can try my best to improve, or alternatively try to find creative ways to change the way I train or swim.

I first found out about former Olympic gold-medallist swimmer Alexander Popov and his coach, Genadi Touretski, and this opened a whole new world of thinking about man's motion as an aquatic animal. I swam more easily and my performance improved. Then I read Terry Laughlin's *Total Immersion Swimming*. I followed his strategy and improved even more. What next? I cannot wait – so I hunt for it.

Such a mindset makes you evaluate everything, as a thinking exercise. How can an airplane seat be improved? What should be done with juvenile delinquents? Is it possible to make a better cover for a laptop? How can an App be made child-resistant? Hence the Porsche Cayenne and the iPhone: it embodies thinking beyond the Good.

Thus you walk through your Empire – watching, thinking and challenging the best on offer, and not just the worst. There are better ideas. We just don't think of them.

The blindness comes from believing that 'good enough' is a timeless statement. It's great for today. Until someone improves on it and you will then have to play catch-up as well as get-ahead. That's a double challenge. Instead of a single hop.

Get the rest of the paid eyes to look at their world in the same way. If the best can be made better, the worst must be extremely easy to improve. Why do we do it this way? What do we do with the outcome? Is it that important? Is this really the best outcome? Question and listen. Raise your standards incessantly and your people will rise to the occasion. They will love being given the chance to think, too.

58.

DISTINGUISH BETWEEN URGENT AND IMPORTANT

Urgent is yesterday's unresolved Important. Spend your effort on what is Important to avoid the tyranny of the Urgent.

The prepared CEO has a to-do list. It's probably long. Mine currently has 768 items, over all aspects of my life. A nightmare of expectations!

The list should be divided in two columns: Urgent and Important. Each column should have a list of to-dos, in descending order from the highest priority to the lowest. The Urgent column will wag its finger at you in admonishment of dereliction of priorities. There should be no items in Urgent. Blank is very good. The Important column should be prioritised from matters which have the highest impact on the enterprise down those which have the lowest impact.

Some things with lower priority will stealthily creep towards their deadline to emerge as Urgent. Best that you deal with or delegate these items early, as it will keep you from getting to the really important Important stuff list.

You will face a crossroad when you get to, say, a hundred items. Either you are immensely important, but useless at execution. Or you are dreaming faster than the rest of your people can run. Either way, it is advisable to have a coffee and a deep discussion with yourself on delegation, staffing, the pace of change, and the advisability of introducing the new against the benefit of perfecting the existing.

Perhaps you will need some help, so make it a beer with someone you trust. Somehow you are failing to take the rest of the crew on the spaceship with you. Reconsider the pace. Pretend, start a new list: Futurama, how *should* your world work.

The proper and effective to-do list is a challenge. I have used a variety of lists and mind maps. The iOS App Clear works best for me. Now, if I can only get the programmers to make the six changes that will perfect it …?

59.

THE ONE-CHANCE RULE

You're in your current position for a good reason. The last incumbent of the chair in which you are resting so comfortably is no more, probably for a good (if unspoken) reason.

At some stage in your tenure, there will be a Great Reckoning, and you will have to regroup and refocus the energies of everyone towards a new point on an ever-shifting horizon. If you're like most of us, you came through the door with a crisis in full swing. Whether or not this was fair, you will have been given an extremely tight deadline in which to blow reveille and point the way. You were expected to, and appointed to, perform the miracle, with perhaps an extremely limited knowledge of the industry, no working knowledge of the staff's capabilities, nor the real factors that lead to this crisis point, marked 'X' on your map.

Yet you said "Yes!" to the package. To the status. To all the irrational things on which an uninformed wannabe (sounds familiar?) bases life-changing decisions. Been there, done that, too.

Let's assume you pulled it off, to the great surprise and delight of all. No sweat. Drinks all round, please barman! Excellent. As the proverb goes: even a blind pig can find an acorn once in a while. Which you did. Now it's time to make sure you do not have to repeat the exercise. The next time you will know enough of what you risked to become trapped in paralysis by analysis. Or even worse: you will fail.

There are not many ready hole-in-one shots in the championship golfer's shot selection. You need to make sure you never need one again. You have proved your worth around that Death's Bend, so now let everyone get their breath back and drive slower and more responsibly, while the adrenaline subsides. Those on the payroll hoped for a miracle and here you are, whizz-kid and all that. Just don't try to cash in on that adulation too soon. Steady on. Small adjustments. Try to manage, not to lead too much.

The One-Chance rule may come later than on day-one. For example, your selection as CEO, following the departure of a Giant in the Industry, was intended to keep his legacy alive, by not doing things differently from the recipe he concocted, tried and proved. The people need the same reassurance, too.

When Armageddon creeps up, you will have a reservoir of good faith and trust – all hinging on your decisions. Rally the troops and announce the plan. Just One Chance – that is all you have to get it right. The enthusiasm to change course when plan#1 fails …is at the square root level. So get it bang on target. First time. A hole-in-one.

60.

Asking is better than telling. Requesting is more effective than commanding

Isn't this obvious? Let your feminine side through. Lady CEOs included.

To ask a question is an open invitation for a proper response. Your infallibility can be tempered. A flat "No!" response after a command has been issued means war, or worse, as it could lead to subversion. Asking requires commitment, not obedience. This is a big difference. By asking, you are actively listening. How does this work?

You, in asking mode: "Can we have the report later today for my review tonight, please?"

"It's not ready yet".

"What parts are not ready yet?"

"Balance sheet needs some work. It's the asset amortization table that's tough."

"Great. Just get me the Income Statement, Cash Flow and Tax Schedule, then. Please give me an ETA on that table."

Game over.

When you say "May I?", or "Could you please?" and the like, it may be seen as a steely-eyed rattler hypnotising the rat. You are putting gloss on the obvious. Great manners will get you on the dance floor, along with a promise of reciprocity, and develop your capacity to understand situations while remaining unflinching on results. Once there, you can learn the steps and so be one step ahead. Stay there.

Don't criticise. Improve. Your delivery is too often the tool that opens the door to understanding, acceptance and action. Hey, you could learn something new every day, as well. Sometimes two things on a good day. Your people are dying for a chance to teach you.

61.

BE ACCOUNTABLE IN THE OPEN

Be responsible. Take blame. Share credit. Plant ideas. Praise openly. Evaluate in private. Expect no public accolades and don't strive for them either. Yearn only for the private satisfaction of a job well done.

Great. Now that you can handle your own kids this way, do the same in the office.

Few will realise just how many mistakes you make. How many calls which you have had to make were closer to marginally good than to a Nobel Prize standard. How many undone things creep around the well-hidden bottom of the pile of your to-do list that stretches well beyond a few pages?

Still they suspect that you are generally plagued by the same insecurities, syndromes and advancing age as all others. What they don't have is your resilience, your never say die spirit, the entrenched credo from Calvin Coolidge – the famous "Press-on!" speech which I mentioned earlier. Here's an extract in case you don't have it at hand:

> *"Nothing in the world can take the place of persistence.*
> *Talent will not; nothing is more common than unsuccessful men with talent*
> *Genius will not; unrewarded genius is almost a proverb.*
> *Education will not; the world is full of educated derelicts.*
> *Persistence and determination alone are omnipotent.*
> *The slogan Press On! has solved and always will solve the problems of the human race."*

You will have to show your human side and to show that you are essentially a humble guy with luck on his side and a generous allocation of smarts, too.

The best way is to account openly for the almost-great decisions. Ask for feedback. After all, you're scouting for your successor, too.

62.

UNDERSTAND RULES *VS* PRINCIPLES

As you are the CEO, it's your desk where the buck stops. Regardless of who it was that screwed up. Compliance is the latest bureaucratic disease foisted on the free spirits who live and die by commerce.

Hence you will be well advised to know the regulations and the rules of your industry, your tax code and your country's laws. There are innumerable of these. Your Legal Counsel is on standby. Not always to guide, but usually to extricate your troubled enterprise from doing a Bad Thing. There are no excuses, as I discussed in the earlier 'Events vs Patterns' section. The law is always a black-and-white world.

Still, we prosper and keep out of trouble by keeping to the right principles.

A phrase which comes to mind is: "Doing the right things and doing things right." Sunshine is the best disinfectant, meaning all transactions must be transparent.

Your principles must be widely known and well understood. We meet the Gods of the crossroads a hundred times every day. With our adherence to the right and correct principles, the deities may continue to smile upon our choices. There would be very little time, or need, to rush back to check the laws and regulations with every decision.

Any fool can make a rule. Most fools abide by them. You don't like a regulation or idiotic compliance issue? Agitate for its change. There are few brave souls out there with the stamina and inclination to manifest their lives in the way they first envisaged. You should be one. So don't sit on your talents.

The world lives by the rules of nature and men are sifted by their reciprocity and consideration. Laws outside of this are inherently unfair and it's your job to match these with your well-versed business philosophy and the strength of your convictions. You must be guided by principles. Laws and rules should not constrain your efforts, unless there is deficiency in either.

Should you adhere to the spirit or the letter of the law?

In some countries, the ethos is that everything is legal unless some law prohibits it. In others the envelope is not pushed in that way. If you are in captivity to the former, your competition may use loopholes – this is decidedly unfair. Ultimately you serve customers whose trust you earn by doing the right things – and, of course, by fearing no-one.

63.

Get familiar with big numbers

Your business and industry will have some pretty large numbers floating around. A familiarity with, and ease of understanding, big numbers will add a proper perspective and some advantage to your analysis of, and dealings in, your industry.

Expanding your growth rate will lead to big numbers. When will you have to recruit the right new staff to cope with the additional business? A 7% fall in margin could have devastating effects over five years, if not countered soon. When is the crisis due? What will it mean three quarters hence? The market is expanding by 4% per annum. Funding the advertising needed to exceed this growth will have knock-on effects. What is the ratio of advertising to growth for your competitors?

What effect would a saving of $100k per month have on the size of our dividends over the next three years?

What is the value of retaining a customer over ten years? What is the payback on growth of a 10% price reduction?

These are not accounting terms. These are the sensitivities involving big numbers. List the things that may influence your decisions and calculate the possible large-number consequences. When these numbers are in your lexicon, the opportunities for their implementation can be recognised and pounced on. Your senior staff should also translate the impact of their decisions into large numbers and share their insights. Growing larger is the result of decisions made, not of decisions forfeited.

Your estimation skills must be practised so they become second nature, too. Every time you ask a question or gauge an outcome, you must have already formulated a clear and close-to-correct estimate. The answer to the question must confirm your hunch or mensuration. Never walk into it cold. The answer you are being given might be completely wrong and you would be the fool who accepted it. Think Reinhart & Rogoff's miscalculated submissions on "Austerity" and shudder. Practise this at every opportunity.

Soon your grasp of events, cash levels and other knowables will get closer and closer to the correct answer. Guess how inspiring it is when the boss plunks down a figure before he asks, and is vindicated? Priceless.

64.

YOUR VISION MIGHT NOT BE THEIR VISION YET

Many things are desirable. Few things are feasible, given that time, money, expertise and the will to conclude are usually in short supply. So where should the CEO hang his target? That to which he aspires, his dream and vision for his enterprise?

The world of positive thought is well debunked by Barbara Ehrenreich in *Smile or Die*. The overhang of the ridiculous mesmerisation of goals by 'positive thinking' is that goals become undoable, unreachable and sometimes pure fantasy.

The central tenet of Shinto is finding **the way**. It is not in setting goals, but in finding the correct way of doing things that will lead down a road. Where the score may be taken from time to time. Targeting a 14% return on investment growth per annum is surely the result of doing things differently. Let's take the cart and put it behind the horse. Reducing the spread of activities, selling more of our best product via a structured referral method. These are the actions connoting **the way**. You will need a philosophy, a vision to back it up.

Perhaps it echoes the golfer's aim to play perfect golf. It may be to unlock the efficiencies, through your people. Somehow, you need to find the lantern to illuminate the path that you will trample in the tall grass. This will guide you to act in **the way** and these steps by the steed will pull the cart along. Why end up at 15%? A lot more is possible if the cart is pulled by a horse that knows the road, guided by a lantern holder who knows the right direction.

It is, of course, true that many – if not most – people are decidedly more inspired by **goals** than by **ways**. So you need to hang a pointer on a tree, to visibly point the direction to destinations along **the way**. Let's reach our goal of 15 debtors' days. Let's get to a rate of closing 75% of sales proposals. Get 15 prospects per week per person. These goals can be repeated by more people. The bigger prize of a rewarding career in a successful company is an accumulation of these small visions and achievements.

Articulate your vision incessantly. The walls have ears. The people too. They must become familiar with your vision before they can trust it. Only after you have won their trust will they think of acceptance and change.

Once it becomes **our** vision, it may become invincible. Careful here, you do not want to mould them to be your clones, in what Adam Smith called a Man of Systems. Your chessmen are diverse and fulfil their roles in their own way. Its where you want to head to that's important.

To create a vision, contrast it with reality. This will define your problem! The vision is the solving of the problem. People can relate to this better than nonsense such as a mantra which goes: to be the best in everything we touch.

Thus **our** vision can be moulded, tempered, changed, improved. It is supported by every player with his measurable and somewhat-stretched contribution target. Every step can be taken in tandem, like the rhythm of a tug-of-war team. Making minimal effort to secure maximum results, without distraction. If they get this right, they are on their **way**.

65.

YOUR MOST IMPORTANT ACTIONS, IN ORDER

1. To manifest, grow, adapt and preach the common vision.
2. To develop, tool up and then motivate your teams to achieve the common goal. **Our** goal.
3. To solve the insoluble, often escalated, problems. Don't just manage them. Get rid of them.
4. To make rain when and where it's needed.
5. *Simplicate* everything. Don't complicate things.

These may sound a little like pulpit vision from some get-rich-quick book. They are not. Without the unified **us** of an oiled, waxed and Teflon-covered horde of Vikings, how would you be able to storm and hold Ireland when you are only a small band?

Our goal, then, is easy. It derives from that of the Vikings: Rape. Pillage. Get Rich. Repeat.

The modern day version of this is: Sell. Deliver. Collect. Repeat.

All too often, people in the organisation are **busy**. They **work**, often staring at a screen for hours while they try hard to look as if they are typing or thinking. This is the Viking equivalent of day-dreaming. What they need to do is **business**, not **work**. **Business** is what the common goal is about: to sell, deliver, and so on.

Their jobs are to make this a reality, to manifest your goal from a common idea. Or else you will have dissent and a crew bent on doing the wrong things while the coast is clear for plunder. It is counterproductive and an evil thing to let their ideas, attention and efforts wander across vistas of their own making. Get them to con-centrate.

It still boils down to the Head Viking needing to lead the charge. Nowadays #1 is all too often ensconced and entrapped in the C-Suite, the one part of the office with the extra-plush carpets. As if a raid could be successful by remote control! The troops need to see you in front from time to time, especially during the tricky times. When the clouds need to be seeded and the ranks need to be united.

At the most critical times you will have to step up to the plate and swing for the rafters. You had better not miss. You are not the best-paid player because of your reputation alone. You need to be able to whip up the home-run when all seems lost. That is how you earn your keep.

In order for others to follow your magnificent example of walking on hallowed water, *simplicate* everything so that it can be ingested, understood and repeated. Grip the Bat. Take the Right Stance. Eyes on the Ball. The whole sequence. This flows all the way down to how the laundry is done. To get that crisp, professional crease in that awesome uniform.

Your most appreciated asset is considerate, productive, supportive, inter-personal **time**. It's the lubricant between people and people, and people and tasks.

Get to grips with ruthlessness. Trade where necessary. Plunder where possible. These are the rules your opposition plays by. So if you can't be reckless, make good defences to keep them at bay.

We went through an ISO 9001 exercise and found we had more than 800 processes. This was after 15 years of *simplicating* everything. We're now down to 200, across all disciplines and there's a pruning and rethink challenge that permeates our business. Not 'being busy', not wasting effort, but helping towards the instilled goal. Swords sharpened? Check. Bear shirts on? Check. OK, let's then roll with minimum effort, berserkers.

66.

STEER YOUR BUSINESS THE WAY YOU FLY A PLANE

Fly it. Don't let it fly you. Correct it often and early. Great advice from my friend Johann van Huyssteen, a pilot and entrepreneur attorney. Nothing begets resentment and anger, disappointment and loss of confidence, as much as a sudden jerk back to an old direction after everyone has been enjoying the unintended benefits of a new shortcut that at first went unchallenged. That's why you need a standard and agreed maximum deviation from all outcomes, from sales achieved to rings allowed at the switchboard before there is an answer.

If you cannot measure it, you cannot manage it. If you do not measure it, you do not manage it. If you do not manage it, you cannot improve it. Or worse: keep it on course. Get a proper dashboard, accessed by all, every day. One that shows the impending wrath of the C-Suite if things get out of kilter. That way, everyone keeps tabs on everyone else and the tsunamis can be spotted early – for corrective, guided adjustments.

Your well-developed golf skills should be a lesson here. How small is the change of angle of the club on the golf ball that either makes a magnificent fairway shot or a 'mullion' shout? It is *fractions* of a degree, Tiger. Your consistencies in hitting gentle shots that are well-aimed outweigh the rippers that *may* end up an Albatross, but more often hang around your neck in failure.

Easy does it, all the time. There's a co-pilot who needs to learn to fly too. So hand over the stick often. Like an old-fashioned guild master, you need to certify the end of an apprenticeship and the start of a new, improved working life and the promotion to something better.

67.

IT IS FAR EASIER TO LEARN FROM YOUR MISTAKES THAN FROM YOUR SUCCESSES

When evaluating a success or failure, consider the source. Was it because of your efforts, or in spite of them?

Few of my peers can distinguish their own PR from reality as far as their success is concerned. Often their wives have a better story to tell about it. Experience is the name we give to our mistakes. We fret and dissect, regret and admonish ourselves to never repeat the same mistake again. Success is alluded to and rewarded. Its origins are generally kept a mystery. There is no pressure on the superstar that did the impossible to come clean about his real method.

The claim that something was easy to accomplish is always easily swallowed. We applaud the modest "Aw, shucks!" response of the victor. Proper analysis of which factors triggered each of the succeeding steps is almost never done as a rule. It is as if the magic spell will be broken when the luck is understood.

However, such analyses are vital and must be embarrassingly candid. This is not easy, but then we are not cheerleaders. We are engineers who must measure and test; coaches who need the slow replay; and judges of what elements of the confluence between what the customer wanted and what the enterprise offered gelled at the exact right moment.

You may be shocked at how often things happen in spite of our best efforts, not necessary because of them. The hot buttons of every customer remain mysterious – even after we have accidently bumped them in the right order. Most customers cannot give a cogent and rational explanation of exactly when and why the buying decision was reached and when it was – the order in which the fireworks went off.

Learning is a difficult process. Often things we already know must be un-learned, to allow the new ideas to spread like ivy up the tree of knowledge. The same rambler may be pulled down shortly and plan C then promoted as the newest, latest solution. And so on. A beginner's mindset is a necessity if you want to make sense of the irrational and uninformed random walks.

Learn from your outcomes, whether they are successes or otherwise. Cultivate an ongoing appreciation of the multi-pronged attack and where Pareto often weaves its magic. This will become your enterprise's intellectual property. How you persuaded the customer to trust you.

68.

WHEN EVALUATING A COURSE OF ACTION, ASK TWO OPPOSING QUESTIONS
"WHY SHOULD I?" THEN: "WHY SHOULD I NOT?"

The answers are not mirror images: they are complementary, not opposing.

It is revealing how the human mind works and how we have learned to rationalise, emphasise and defend the first ideas that pop into that vacant space. Especially so in a contest, such as a meeting or strategy session. Here's what you need to do …

List the reasons for why something should be done, based on the facts. Then list the reasons for why it should *not* be done, based on the same facts. An interesting pattern will appear. This exercise does not necessary lead to the drawing up of two opposing lists. It will add perspective to the question that always preceded your Business School case studies: what should you do?

The more facts you have, the better the basis for a decision. If you get a little stuck in the participation exercise, Edward de Bono's 'Six Thinking Hats' and 'Six Action Shoes' – as described in his books -- are great icebreakers and very good to gain facts and perspectives.

As the leader, you need to get the best thinking processes going. Watch Henry Fonda in *Twelve Angry Men* for a bit of humble pie and great argumentation and persuasion.

In discussion of all the factors for and against a decision – all the **why's** and **why not's** – there will hopefully be a number of differing opinions. As clever as you are, you will glean the facts, present these and then answer the question of whether to go or to stay.

69.

SOME ACTIONS ARE INCREMENTAL; SOME ARE TRANSFORMATIONAL

Let's harp on the 80/20 principle some more. Within the 20%, there would be another 80/20 too, and that's where these second-generation questions become interesting.

Let's get back to the Reasons for Success. The second generation's 20% should be more revealing than the first. Moira and Corene are the salespeople who bring in the most business. The bulk of the business emanates from the mining sector. The mining houses where we have had success make their decisions at the mine site. They are not made at the company headquarters. Moira will routinely make a three-hour sojourn to the desolate countryside where the mining operations are located.

Is she that good, or are they just glad to see someone from the city making an effort?

What can we do that's transformational? We sold telecommunications services that were cheaper than those of the incumbent. When Chris, the buyer for one of our customers, said his boss would be pleased if we could quantify this, we started printing a 'Saving Cheque' every month, with the exact value of the savings down to two decimals. We started generating this for his company and he added it to his monthly report. The first cheque was for about $40 000.

What we did next was transformational. We generated a report in graphic format showing *where* we had saved him money. With the cheque, we automatically produced this report, in PDF, for all our customers, as part of our invoice run. Twelve years later, Chris' office has a wall plastered with our cheques. He has saved over $6 million, even though he was paid only about 5% of that as salary.

His profile as a money generator in a budget-conscious industry is safe.

Strive for the transformational. What are the things emanating from your successes that you can do elsewhere to transform your business and even your industry? It may take a lot of ideas, time and frustration, but finding the diamond in the pile is more than worth the hunt. It becomes essential to your business.

Don't just manage in paradigms and clichés such as: 'known knowns.' It is evident that many CEOs have a limited Bag of Tricks and, like street magicians, fall back on what pleases the crowds. You need a bigger repertoire and you first need to create it and to test it, in non-critical areas. Sales slump? The knee-jerk knowns are price cuts, cost cuts and lay-offs; like a Dr Seuss on management. You are in charge here. Where's plan B and why didn't it kick in automatically? Think transformational!

70.

DON'T FALL INTO THE TRAP OF JUST FAVOURING THOSE PEOPLE YOU LIKE

Like = Good. Don't Like = Bad. That may be your first instinct, but it is wrong. Better to instead evaluate objectively, especially if it involves a person. We are human, self-opinionated and value our own judgement immensely, often over everything else. No wonder we bat so badly in business. How can we be wrong? Or contemplate the admission of such errors? It's almost unthinkable.

It takes some practice to separate the person from the idea, or the behaviour from the benefit. We make decisions based on emotion. We rationalise later. We apologise to no-one. After all, didn't circumstances change since the decisions were made?

The caution here is about your liking or disliking the person and then basing your decision on that feeling. How can good things come from people you dislike? However, it is sounder to differentiate between whether you *trust* someone and whether you *like* them. An ideal package scores high on both, but the sucker punch is also coated like this: your dislike should work in your favour. Your vigilance and focus will be fighting your judgement to prove you wrong.

For every person you dislike, there may well be others who hold the opposite view about them. You just don't have the key to unlock the relationship, yet.

Tackle the benefits offered. Find out if your people can work with the unpalatable person whom you dislike, should a professional relationship follow. Is the supplier trustworthy? If you immediately give in to your dislike, you may make the wrong call. Your dislike may lead to a distorted rationalisation of why the supplier is no good.

It works in the opposite direction as well. 'Like' can be dangerous. I fear the day a Nicole Kidman look-alike breezes in with a briefcase full of snake oil, because I may be doomed.

At the same time, this logic works in an upwards direction, too. Don't confuse respect for your position with people actually liking you. It may well be that they don't like you. It's the rank they respect. Or fear. Beware of the uncomfortable familiarity this may cause. How can they deny your request, or invitations from you that are not work-related?

As a rule – and your culture may be the exception – I never socialise with any of my co-directors, employees, suppliers or customers, outside of workweek breakfasts, lunches or business chats over coffee. Their lives are tough enough keeping you happy or expecting your magic to rub off. So keep away.

Your personal life remains a closed book to them and they are free to speculate on it. Theirs are the same, except for your interest in how their kids are performing. If they want you to know about their divorce or mishaps they will tell you. If you ask, they will be compelled to blurt out their secrets. So don't.

Each of your colleagues will have their own opinion about you. The only opinions that really matter are how your customers view the enterprise.

71.

KNOW THE DIFFERENCE BETWEEN BEING CLEVER AND BEING WISE

You will constantly be judged by your mistakes, not by your achievements. It's that single dropped pass at the crucial point in the game that will define your life forever. So it is in the wider world. Your success and brilliance are only tolerated. Your disasters are fêted by a populace steeped in the laws of nature. The vanquished lion does not receive a long-service award. His cubs are routinely killed by the victor.

Someone voiced a rule: "Being clever is knowing what to say. Being wise is knowing whether or not to say it." As an ex-wiseass and politically-deaf youth, I keep wondering how many great opportunities I have screwed up by being forthright, bluntly truthful and damn clever. Probably many.

It is limiting, however, to wholly withhold your wisdom from the rest of the world. Instead of issuing clever opinions, why don't you start a newsletter? Meanwhile, much has been said and written about good listening skills. Such skills, coupled with a clever and humble questioning style, may make the world's oyster open up a few more degrees and can add somewhat to your encyclopaedic version of everything.

Hear what is not being said. One day you may find someone who is good and clever in questioning you, too, and through such a meeting, soulmates may be born.

It is the rushed assumption that may lead you into the mistake. It is the considered question that may rescue you before that slip can occur. Being wise is a judgement. Being clever is a performance. Sitting at the head of your massive boardroom table, you would rather receive a sage nod from a wise executive than a clever rant from a Young Turk. Cultivate the Young Turks too.

Always value experience over schooling. Schooling and thinking give rise to questions, even fresh questions. Experience, in contrast, brings answers that may be tempered, but answers that once proved true in the real world. Every day you start anew, as with a fresh cricket match. Your batting has to be immaculate. Your fielding needs to be even better. Your team players should be chosen for their excellence under duress and their ability to win. Get wise.

72.

Polish your brinkmanship skills

Combat is the last solution, after diplomacy has failed. At some point you will make a stand, and if you do, it needs to be defended. Your skill at **brinkmanship** determines the extent to which you can defend your stance, and at what cost you are willing to do so.

The art of diplomacy is often and widely disregarded at executive level. Often performance alone is touted as the true worth of the CEO. Business is not a one-dimensional world.

So there are a manifold other traps to negotiate, most of them hidden, and they may seem unfair to the outside observer.

If you want to beat a dog, any stick will do. When the Board wants to stick it to you, any excuse will do. The confrontation is usually yours for the losing if your diplomatic skills are not sharp. So, what should you do?

You would have initiated private meetings with individual Board members, to bounce your new ideas off their accumulated wisdom. You would have aired frustrations that they could help alleviate. You will have expressed your thanks for their support in past Board meetings. You will have shared private insights, understood the interrelationships without asking and will have assumed that you're the Patsy for their games. Of course they have no secrets from each other. They deal in information and opinions.

You will have acted wisely. Board members can be fired only for dissent from those who selected them and then voted them on the Board in the first place. You want to get the message across that you understand their concerns and are pursuing their agenda as well as yours. As the Action Man.

There will be times when a sudden line in the sand will be drawn, and your choice to concede or confront will be tested, sometimes for real. A bullet that establishes a base trajectory – what is euphemistically called a sighter – may be fired in your direction. This might be to test your resolve and your skills in handling conflict.

In much the same way, you may recall that an unexpected recruitment call came just as you were setting in. The caller offered you double your new salary. You batted that away nicely, stating for the record how extremely dedicated you were and how determined to see through the current challenge. "Thank you. Please don't bother to call again." You passed that test. If you didn't, the knives would already have been out for you.

You have a single opportunity to set the bar on **brinkmanship**. How high do you value the good of the company, and especially its shareholders, over your relationship with the Board? You need to go to the extreme, based on principle. You need to stare down the lion and his mock charge. When the real trouble comes, the Board will have a measure of just how big the fight will have to be to get the stick to land on the dog. Good luck.

73.

GET TO THE TRUTH

When evaluating the quality of an argument, do remember that if the argument is weak, the arguer may well hide this by Shouting like Hell!

Truth is an elusive concept and there are a few human traits that will disclose it. Remember that you will be the last person to know what really goes on in the enterprise. This is because all the info you receive may well be politically packaged for someone's benefit and it's not necessarily for yours. Your poor PA, if you deem yourself important enough to have a gatekeeper, has an unenviable job. She knows, and may not want to tell you, what she suspects is going on. Even that may not turn out to be the whole truth.

A good rule is that the person showing the most emotion is usually bluffing. If a customer is Shouting like Hell at your staff, it is a reliable indication of who's in the right here. Perhaps he has already signed up with somewhere else and is now blaming your product or your staff to justify his move.

A further rule is to ask the question and judge the answer by its verbosity. True answers are generally short, to the point, and offer no justification or blame. "Did that?" "No." "Why not?" That's a good dialogue. Be suspicious of an answer filled with lots of emotion and detail. Such as: "Of course not. I would never do a thing like that. What do you think I would do that for …?" Let's call this the One Breath Answer rule, because short answers are usually true and wise.

Think *cui bono*. Who benefits? Now that this has happened, who stands to gain? This is a tool to dissect world politics, false-flag ventures and why the coffee supplier was changed without due authorisation.

Beware the Hegelian trap: a preconceived solution that needed a situation to be devised for it to emerge as the answer. Few of us ever studied the Marxist dialect, but it is diabolically effective. Want to invade a country? Let's set up the rebels, vilify the legitimate response and that then gives us the excuse to move in. That's pure Hegel. Watch out.

You may be played in this way too. Want to change the coffee supplier? Let's give the incumbent an unreasonable deadline so we cause a delivery shortage. Hegel is the outcome.

Many situations are set up to give a predetermined outcome. Do not get fooled by the closed question leading to the closed answer.

74.

THINK CONTINUOUSLY ABOUT THE CHALLENGES

Opportunity is often where you look for it. If you do not know what you are looking for, you will not find it. If you are not looking, it won't find you either.

We often see and find what we are looking for. If we are not knowingly looking for something, that something will be filtered out and someone else may find it, correctly identifying it as a brilliant opportunity.

If sleep is an underrated activity, then dreaming is off the scale of neglect. If you do not have a head full of questions, showering will be a simple act of hygiene instead of a steam-filled strategy session with the wisest guy you know. A journey as a passenger would be marking time, instead of triggering a burst of creativity.

The process works as follows: ask yourself a relevant question. Write it down. Formulate it properly and simply. Give your subconscious the time to unravel it and constitute an answer. The answer will be pretty simple. This means that the heart of the trick is to ask a simple question.

If you think continuously about the challenges, your subconscious can get to grips with the answers.

You should have many hours every night for your ever-awake reticular activation system to send its librarian to the accumulated files, under 'W' for wisdom. Then to hurry back with a three-word missive. It works like this …

Q: How shall we differentiate our product now that it has been simplicated?
A: Box it.

Q: Should we buy the Eastern Cape business and bid against Dirk?
A: Finance him.

With the right set of questions at the back of your mind you will be alert to the answers and opportunities. Ask questions that seem irrelevant at the time, but may turn out to be decisive.

The unconscious mind is supportive of your ongoing quest for answers and it should be harnessed. What's the last thing you tell yourself when you are about to doze off? Make it one of the questions that you have written down. The answer will generally come. The timing is uncertain, but it will only come once. Arriving at an 'ah-ha!' moment is a wonderful feeling. Treasure and develop it.

75.

Making trouble

You may have a life goal of doing well. That's laudable and great. The world needs successful people doing good things for the people close to them and for others.

There is a neglected side of doing good, to which few aspire, and which only some have the strength to shoulder. That's making trouble!

> *The only thing more worthwhile than doing good where good is needed is making trouble where trouble is needed.*

Making trouble requires a particular attitude, because you need to be brave, not fearless. Doing good? Well that requires little courage. Especially if it means just dishing-out money instead of your most precious asset – your own time.

Making trouble requires all three of these elements: time, money and courage. Doing good makes few enemies. Making trouble sets the world right but will pit many people against you. By doing good deeds, you stroke your ego. If you do the right things this will tick off other people who were getting away with the misdeeds.

Still your shoulders are wider than your grin and your thighs are thicker than your neck. You may be the type of person on whom society relies. The sheriff who can confront evil and the patriot who takes to heart the Edmund Burke quote: "The only thing necessary for the triumph of evil is for good men to do nothing". This is a remarkable and true statement from a remarkable man.

You – and those around you – are faced with the Choice of Hercules. Your choice is between the one path of duty or the other of pleasure. The first will lead to strife, hardship and perhaps glory and legacy. The other to worldly ease and comfort, but with an unre-markable life.

How true is your passion for a better future for your progeny? What better way to find out than to stand tall? Trouble will surely find you and then you will know your true worth. Through acquiring the wisdom to know that adversity does not build character. It merely reveals it. Dare to make a stand on the line you have drawn in the sand – in line with your own conscience. Then defend it with everything you have. In such a way, heroes are born.

76.

TEMPTATION

You are probably very, very good at what you're doing. So don't bet the house on gaining an easy, extra under-the-counter percentage.

The temptation is often there to take a little shortcut, to sail a little closer than necessary to the wind. In a way that would elicit a disappointed headshake from the chairman. You may tell yourself that the Law is an Ass and it's geared more to dissuasion than to punishment. Of course, you've always been lucky …

Still, there are 10 000 ways to screw up that you've never heard of. If you want to skirt the unmentionable, then get professional crooked advice. Do not do an amateur dabble. There are enforcers making career advancements from joyriding idiots. Go very bad or stay straight.

In short: rather resist the temptation to follow anything other than the straight and narrow. You are breathing exalted air and you may have an army of loyal-to-death captains already smelling that bonus if you just say the word.

Your loyal cadres won't go to jail for you. They won't take the blame or defend you to the death. If the head honcho slips, it's the age-old adage of: "The King is dead; long live the King."

Perhaps you have seen the consequences of others' foolish actions being reported in the press, knowing full well that maybe 99% of all that is actually going on will never surface. There are so many underhand, corrupt, crazy things surrounding you. Surely a little misstatement in valuation wouldn't hurt anyone? Or an over-optimistic view of a contingent liability, or an upcoming lawsuit that may need extra provision? You may stay true to the truth and pay the price of missing your targets. These lapses are small temptations that can form a habit once you have crossed that line in the sand.

Heaven knows what will happen below decks if the word spreads that the captain drinks in private.

Epictetus' final day in Rome started when a fellow philosopher ran in with the news that Domitian had mandated that all philosophers must cut off their trademark beards or face banishment.

The lament was: "What shall I do, Epictetus? What will you do?"
The reply came: "You will cut your beard and I shall have my lunch."
"Why must I cut it and you won't?"
"Because you considered it."

Such is the Stoic mind, the **way**. This is the perfect example of the link between thoughts, actions, habit, life and legacy. Epictetus was banned from Rome and was then lost to history. His example is immutably perfect. Yours should be, too.

77.

PEAKING

We have all seen child prodigies and witnessed the uneven hand of nature that dumped effusive talents on a single individual. It was so unfair to the rest of us. Well, our generous applause drowned out the petty jealousies, didn't it?

Now you're King of the Hill and you probably weren't born there either. Perhaps you were the prodigy or the red-haired stepchild. This does not matter anymore. Welcome to the Peaking Theory!

Everyone peaks sometime in life, but not everyone traces a lofty arc through the heavens. An exceptional few may peak more than once. You have a choice on when you would want to peak. So when will it be?

Many of our contemporaries peaked in high school, never again climbing the podium of exultation, or waving down a crowd of admirers. School is a small world with a limited number of age-related competitors. Others peaked a bit later, and became the Big Man on Campus. These were rarely the school stars. Then onto real life, where the competition is open to all ages and all countries. This is the Olympics of Life.

If you kept your best for this crowded run, then congratulations. Peak when you're in your early 60s, because that will give you a long and interesting life of continuous achievement to hone your way.

The late Fred du Plessis, who became Chairman of Sanlam, a large South African insurance company, was at one time a lecturer at my Alma Mater. He continued to visit annually to motivate the newly elected Student Council. I followed his advice ...

> *"Don't get serious about life until you're 30. You have energy and no experience. Get experience.*
>
> *Decide what you're good at between 30 and 40 and work*

at it.

At 40, decide what you're going to be when you're grown up and then concentrate your energy and experience on it.

At 50 you will have the wisdom of choices."

He didn't elaborate further. This worked for me, albeit in an age that has long gone. This Peaking Theory grew from living this life and marking passage in achieving my way. I followed my dream and celebrated my third Stock Exchange listing the day before I turned 50. I still intend to peak at 70. My investment in something better is continuing, I have another listing lined up, and a first international venture is being rolled out. The same target-setting should hold true for you.

Your tenure will be limited. The average for a hired CEO is about three to five years. What will be next for you? Where will you be when you intend to peak? What will it take? It's time to decide. Then pace yourself. Life is a marathon, not a sprint.

78.

NURTURE YOUR SUCCESSORS

In observing all of the above, make sure you are developing your successors. Your vision is linked to the **how** and your example to the **way**. Those in charge of the spades at work must understand your thinking. Anticipate it, like the perfect horse in JD Salinger's tale of Duke Mu of Chin, in *Raise High the Roof Beam, Carpenters*. Your grooms must know the thinking of the jockey, understand and display the qualities you embody, require and reward.

Few people have ever worked physically hard. We're past the age of farm holidays. You can spot the diamonds from the speed with which they finish easy tasks and the speed at which they start off on difficult tasks. Treasure these diamonds and point them towards the stars. Ask them about the achievements that got them to this point. You may be surprised at the endurance of the human spirit.

Some are Stationary Target people. Others are Moving Target people, those who can adapt and re-aim in mid-stride. This second group comprises your shock troops, who can be pressed into service while the shock waves still paralyse the emotionally weak. Remember the effects of severe stress? You need to identify and nurture those quick responders. Those who will take up the slack in inevitable crises.

From their multiple tours as security operatives in Iraq, my battle-hardened friends have two lessons for survival. Choose the like-minded colleague for your squad who remains unfazed by flying lead and choose a proper rifle from the Springfield Armoury, as all rifles are not created equal.

Pass on your organisation's crucial lessons to those who take up the new positions. These lessons are learned the hard way and must permeate your enterprise down to the DNA, through the marrow of its bones. Everyone can drive a car in a straight line, but the value lies in those who can negotiate dangerous turns without losing much speed.

Can anyone ever fully understand human intent, reactions, motivation and loyalty? This is all the more reason to study and understand them, as an ongoing student of human life on earth. Then share your insights.

Keep offering your people those opportunities which bring the most out of them. Matching ability with opportunity. Keep tabs on the speed and success of progress. Find the single thing that oils the gears best in each and every individual and department. Be the hero by undoing the shackles and reminding them of their freedom to do proper business. Now you can relax while the race to replace you is in full swing.

79.

PAYING YOURSELF

You will probably have one chance at glory. Any second attempt at a turnaround will discreetly trigger recruitment ads like those that you first saw, and which led to your application to climb to the top of the ladder.

There is a limited number of reasons why a new CEO is needed, with all the complications, emotional trauma and risk this entails.

Congratulations. It is your turn to pick up the keys, as well as the pieces left lying around. If you are lucky, the incumbent did a sterling job and leaves a hot company instead of a hot seat, without an obvious successor. If your *hamingja*, your Viking Luck, is diminished, you may still shake the hand being outstretched in a warm welcome, but your odds for success are decidedly lower.

The enterprise may be teetering, cashless and in dire need of resuscitation. Or else the founder is stepping up to become Chairman and founder Junior is your new Vice-President. Worse still, the perfectly good enterprise that roared along has sprouted a number of wannabe #1s. They are pretty much taken aback that you obviously conned the Board and charmed yourself into being their superior and they may regard this as merely a temporary setback for them. Boards change. Markets go up and down. You have more or less the same crew on your longship to take on raids and only a single chance at glory.

Apparently the *conjones* in your family are extraordinary and you will happily trade tomorrow's imminent grief for today's title of: 'The Man'.

How do you pay yourself in these troubling circumstances? It grieves me to see the magnificent sums of which obviously self-serving Remuneration Boards deem their CEOs to be worthy. They can be paid at levels which suggest it is the CEO, and not the owners, who takes the enterprise value risk. Which the CEO doesn't. This is a worldwide malaise: the CEO remuneration scorekeeping game, where more is better and therefore status is denoted by pay instead of by results. Some leaders are so poor that all they have is money.

Better that you structure a long-term deal that makes you a humbly paid executive, with stellar payouts when the results surpass the agreed-upon thresholds. Those types of results give rise to bragging rights. Priceless. Everyone should be happier and your worth will be well proven. Take that, young pretenders.

80.

DON'T TAKE YOURSELF TOO SERIOUSLY

The *Dilbert* comic strip by Scott Adams should be required reading every day for everyone in your enterprise. If people recognise anyone resembling the Pointy-haired Boss in your office, then fix it before irreparable shame sets in. Bravo, Scott! You are the world's best campaigner against the stupidity in which management so often cloaks itself.

Regarding your tenure as the personification of the Gift of the Gods to all mankind, remember that you're temporary. They will forget you unless the lament for your departure is like Mark Anthony's funeral oration for Julius Caesar:

"The evil that men do lives after them;
The good is oft interred with their bones."

Best savour the sense of entitlement while you are the saviour of shareholders and the Beacon of Light on the Hill. It is wonderful while the game is in progress, even better if you start the second half and you are not substituted before the game ends in victory, with you as the all-scoring star. Hey, this is the way of all life.

Shuffle off the stage, memories intact and find a new hobby that doesn't require high stakes and which doesn't manipulate people and figures for a living. The stress is over and the heroes fade all too soon. Your legacy is the wisdom, the can-do demeanour and the inspiration you sparked. Legacy is a phrase with a silent "my".

Spend more time at home *right now*. Spend time thinking, but while also enjoying your fast-growing kids and long-suffering spouse. You will never have an opportunity to make-up for lost time, even if you now tell yourself that you will. This is both Important and Urgent. You may not be the hero you think you are to them, although the magnificent way in which you provide for them is some consolation. You may learn the real tenets of management there: frugal economies, 20-year plans and a merciless adherence to standards and outcomes. Thank your spouse for these lessons.

Spend some time with fellow CEOs. Find them, cultivate the friendships of like-minded peers with whom you can share the bragging rights and demonise failures. If wise, they won't comment or judge, but will silently share. That should be your cowboy way, too. To be heard is all you can ask. Advice is not needed. This camaraderie will endure into your post-glory days that we call retirement. That's when the bones can be picked over and you will realise just how lucky you were in many of your decisions and what a charmed life you've led, in spite of your failings and pure idiocy.

All the more reason to play hard, but with perspective. Someone out there is better than you at everything you are doing, but this is your chance to find the limits of *your* talent in conjunction with those you chose to help steer the ship.

Witty and frequent self-deprecation will narrow the distance between you and those who know your failings better than you suspect. You're also human and fallible. You need willing hands to help you up, not shocked faces to stare at your apparent misfortune after a fall.

How would you measure yourself? Simply by whether or not you met your objective. No excuses. At the end of all this, Deepak Chopra best termed the legacy test:

> *"Look for the Goddess of Wisdom and the Goddess of Wealth might find you."*

81.

TEST FOR RANK

You are starting a negotiation. Step one is to evaluate the rank of the team at the opposite end of the table. How much wiggle room do they have? Assess if they are really the ultimate forum for signing off and sealing the deal.

Non-Disclosure Agreements have crossed the table. Now demand that the limit be approved by a Board resolution before you can commence. Of course yours is in the envelope in front of you. This is called a test of rank. It is detestable to go through endless loops of clarification and agreement, just to be told at the last moment that the agreement now needs ratification at another level.

You need to be aligned as well: CEO *vs* CEO. Never you as CEO *vs* their CFO; or your CTO *vs* their Board. Positional power needs to be allocated evenly across the table. Then comes the test:

You test how serious your supplier is taking you, by making unreasonable demands of him. The purpose of the test is to determine whether the team leader opposite can make the call, and if so, then you can revert to reason, argument and the subtleties of negotiation. You are now *mano a mano*: hand to hand with a worthy opponent. Relish it.

82.

RELIGION

There are perhaps five things that contrast religion with business, where Mammon's rules are different and troublesome if they are not well understood.

Firstly, the rules of your enterprise are constant in their daily demands. Not all religious people are constantly religious. Few will bother with saying Grace at the office canteen in the same way as they would do before meals at home. Often prayer is invoked more in times of crisis than during a carefree workday. In contrast, your rules are unrelenting in their application.

The second difference follows from this. Business requires atonement and restitution when rules are broken. There is no universal forgiveness just because it is asked for, sincerely or otherwise. There are big and small sins in business, and accountability cannot be shirked by confession and regret. Religious absolution, in contrast, can be quick, free, and easy to acquire.

Third, love, compassion, humility and subservience are great virtues in religious settings, but not in the cut and thrust of the competitive world of business. Dominance, relentless pursuit and a winner-takes-all approach are standard and expected. Turning the other cheek is a foreign concept in business, reserved for losers. Business is battle and war. The meek may inherit the earth. But not this week.

The fourth difference is that the locus of control in the enterprise is firmly vested in the employee. The required and expected degrees of responsibility and authority cannot be diminished by quoting or blaming an External Force. The Heavens are not responsible for something untoward happening.

Lastly, business in general is based on Protestantism, unfortunately. In most cultures, rich men work less. That's why they wanted to be rich in the first place. Even Cicero proclaimed the dream to become pleasurably idle. Yet we expect the degree of stress, the number of hours in the office, and the sheer effort, to increase with each higher rung we reach on the corporate ladder.

The medieval Catholics had an ethic to share work amongst an increasing number of people, so none would remain without income. The reigning version of capitalism is unrelentingly a religion of the self-sacrificing work ethic, in its liberal, Anglo-Saxon, mould. Admittedly a broad statement.

83.

STAFF RETRENCHMENT RISK AND PROVISION

In a turnaround stage, the one large move that you may want, or at least need to make is to retrench staff. Hopefully you never get there, but the odds favour no-one in this. What kills many turnaround plans is the lack of cash to fund them, as staff severances are not a 90-day rollover item in the budget.

You should always fund the consequences of potential risks, of which retrenchments could be the largest. A little rainy-day cash under the proverbial mattress could prove a lifesaver. So it would be best if you were to set up a retrenchment fund which could finance the retrenching of a third of your total staff. Put it into a money market fund with a 30-day withdrawal notice. The cash needs to be available, but out of daily reach.

The staff risk has an additional dimension. In the risk analysis, your divisional heads need to draw up an Absolutely Worst Case Scenario list, naming everyone who is not critically irreplaceable. You may want to review these lists and adapt them to the real who-gets-the-parachute scenario.

As a rule of thumb, you need to retain one-half to two-thirds of each Division's team, depending on many factors. If your people feel they must keep almost all those currently on their teams, it's time to Pareto everything and then everyone, including those sliding the doomsday lists over the table. You know now which employees are inching towards dead wood, and it's sometimes better to ignite a controlled brushfire in order to prevent a devastating wildfire later.

Domino's Pizza under Tom Monaghan in the early 80s had a policy to fire 20% of all staff on the 1st of April. All levels of April Fool were affected. At 4:00 pm, the Store Managers were thinned out. At 6:00 pm their bosses (the Corporate Area Managers) were likewise culled. By midnight the survivors learned which VPs were being sacked. There was great apprehension, but the levels of performance in the preceding months were something to behold. Predatory, but effective. Such moves were wonderfully effective but would be unthinkable today.

84.

BOARD MEETINGS

Ron Schreuder held the typical SA Breweries (SAB) Company Board meeting perfectly. As previous chairman in the 1970s of Delta, the Rhodesian arm of SAB, he knew his trade, blended politics and efficiency, and elevated it to an art form. His Board meetings lasted 15 minutes, with all items properly attended to.

In Ron's meetings, all items were voted on straight away and all voting was unanimous. The rub lies in that a Board meeting was never intended to be a discussion forum, but a showcase of clearly understood and agreed strategy. Minutes and proposals were circulated in good time. If something had not initially been well understood, or you questioned the proposals, you needed to have cornered the proposer well in advance, to have your toe to toe. If the outcome of this was unsatisfactory, the chairman would have been called in to mediate and to reach a decision, after hearing the arguments.

His call was final, and that's the way everyone voted. Once in a while, there was a ganging-up and serious disagreement, but Ron would not be persuaded democratically. He made the final call on the basis of one principle: what was in the best interest of the company? That is how the votes went, too. Everyone was informed and on board. A wonderful show of unity commenced.

The 1986 Group AGM, chaired by the legendary Meyer Kahn, lasted less than ten seconds. This pervasive culture of SAB probably made Meyer stand up and say words to the effect of: "Ladies and Gentlemen, the Group made wonderful profits this year and I want you to remember that we did so because we paid our people too little."

He sat down to a great hush.

He took only one question and answered: "All expenses have a determined price. Your people do not. If you pay them too little, they will leave. Pay them what they are worth and we won't make a profit. What they are worth is the difference between price and cost. Always remember that."

Lunch was then served to our 150-odd Group directors, subsidiary Boards' directors and executives. A stunning display of a focused Group culture.

The lesson is clear. Pre-meet and pre-digest information in order to make the Unitary Board a reality and strangle the politics at the same time.

85.

HONESTY

My friend Glenn Philips holds the record for 85 combat sorties: the most ever flown in a Mirage fighter. He retired from the Border war and the SA Air Force unscathed and flew commercially for many years before he set up a business marketing a unique building method.

His frustration with the disciples of Mammon was simple: he adhered to the flyboy code and could not understand that others didn't. In flying, everyone had to be honest all the time, or else someone was likely to die. You had to share correct information, truthful feedback and your reputation would vaporise in an instant if you could not be trusted to objectively deal in the truth all the time, every time. You were expected to voice the truth without being asked for it. That is how problems and issues were resolved and how pilots learned about deficiencies where they never expected anything but perfection.

Brutal or undiplomatic? There are an infinite number of things that are deemed correct or good when done by the boss, but unsound when carried out by someone else. Your own creativity may be just the same thing as someone else's inability to follow instructions. Your laudable firmness as CEO is no different to another's dangerous pig-headedness, and so on …

Honesty is not only truth, but also has context. Tolerating double standards is not honesty. Judging people instead of their behaviour amounts to dishonesty. Exceptions, rule-bending, condoning what is wrong, and tolerating improper conduct are all in the same category. How honest should you be before pleading the Fifth Amendment and staying silent?

My general rule in business is to never be dishonest in what I say or what I do. I cloak this in the explicit understanding that my silence implies neither a **yes,** nor a **no**. I might have to do this because I am bound under a Non-Disclosure Agreement, but often I am bound by my conscience, or the trust of another. Or it may simply be that I do not want to answer and nor do I care to speculate or discuss.

I will never say **yes** when the answer is **no** and I don't give partial truths either. That must be made clear, and understood. Perhaps you have a better way that is more diplomatic and acceptable. If I don't first win the trust of people who believe my every word, there would surely be disappointment and tears later.

86.

ETHICS

I do not understand the management concept of **ethics**. In our country, a body called the King Commission recommended that an Ethics Committee should be set up inside companies, to report to the Board. Lists are drawn up of dos and don'ts. The exercise smacks of the mission-vision craze that has gainfully employed many, but in reality has meant as much as the morning mist. What is **ethics** other than a single word: honesty?

This should cut through all kinds of boondoggle and landmines of rules, regulations, acceptable behaviour and the like. Honesty is being true to the person that you want to be despite the person that you are. Honesty is knowing where you stand with others and likewise defines your dependability factor inside the team.

Honesty is giving the value that is expected for the *salarium* bestowed. In all, it reflects the Viking creed to do what's right. Honesty to your own intentions, honestly shaped and aimed, so executed … and so your world is shaped. Honesty is the contract for mutual exchange and the basis on which to judge others. Whatever **ethics** may mean to others, I believe it all boils down to this.

My gripe with the *non-sequitur* of professionalism is similar. I fail to grasp why there would be any other definition of honest dealings and actions. Claiming to be acting as a professional seems to be an affected cloak of impartial, uninvolved sadism. The unemotional doctor pulls the plug professionally. Or, in other words, with some kind of medical/psychological-defined detachment from the situation.

I get the same feeling when confronting a banker or a lawyer – of an invisible screen of protection, notwithstanding the horrors and unjust actions about to be launched. Professional is the sobriquet of a nasty deed done by a soulless functionary. I demand instead to have interaction with flesh, blood and feelings.

87.

COURAGE

There is a great distinction between being brave and being fearless. Beware the man who knows no fear, or at least let it be known that he is tough. Therein lies someone ready to show off a peculiar death wish. He is a gambler bluffing his path to a destiny which involves an inevitable downfall.

The courageous person is the one that, when the situation arises, echoes King Henry's speech before Harfleur so wonderfully described by Shakespeare:

"In peace there's nothing so becomes a man
As modest stillness and humility:
But when the blast of war blows in our ears,
Then imitate the action of the tiger;
Stiffen the sinews, summon up the blood,
Disguise fair nature with hard-favour'd rage;
Then lend the eye a terrible aspect;
Let pry through the portage of the head
Like the brass cannon; let the brow o'erwhelm it
As fearfully as doth a galled rock
O'erhang and jutty his confounded base,
Swill'd with the wild and wasteful ocean.
Now set the teeth and stretch the nostril wide,
Hold hard the breath and bend up every spirit
To his full height."

Here we see an ordinary person roused to make a stand on principle. On something far greater than himself, as opposed to the fearless man showing only himself. Being courageous goes hand in hand with confidence, and these two character traits feed into each other. The happy outcome may be respect, and this is earned not by being someone, but by doing something that requires courage.

Nasty customers will want a piece of your day. Seemingly intractable problems will paralyse people into stupors. Small but threatening things may materialise on otherwise normal days.

This is where you step up to the plate and widen the shoulders. Courage doesn't mean winning. It means stepping out of your bounds into the ancient role of Protector, the prerequisite for Leader. Winning does help, but there's no need to do everything yourself or to hog the accolades. Courage means sharing the praise for good ideas and the benefit derived therefrom. Courage is just as much about taking a stand as it is about sitting down to listen.

My mentor and late philosopher friend Leon Hart says: "*Genius has its limitations but stupidity is boundless.*" Think before you show your hand.

Being courageous is non-negotiable. You will have to confront your fears and meet the expectations that you will help others to confront theirs, whether you think it's necessary or not. You may not shirk this, nor doubt whether you should don the gladiatorial armour. Of all things, you must be seen and known as the one who will take the bullet, ride the tiger, and outwit the Medusa.

The merest hint of cowardice is fatal. If you go down, it must be as you march into battle to the rousing refrain of Bon Jovi's *Blaze of Glory*. Nothing beats a martyr's legacy. Get up on that horse again. Life at the Top can and will be a rough ride. You are one of the chosen few, whose hat is in the ring.

88.

CAPTAINCY

When to lead and when to follow? How far ahead must the leader stay or stray?

The best answer came in a conversation with Francois Pienaar, the captain of the victorious Springbok Rugby team in the 1995 World Cup.

Rugby is a team sport. So is business. The best example of a team acting in unison is a tug-of-war squad. Collectively all of them, in perfect synchronicity, combine their strength.

Francois said that with 14 of your fellow team players on the field, it is vital that each one plays to his potential, or at least to the expected level, during the 80-minute match.

A captain's role is to make sure that every player is playing at full stretch. As the captain, he was able to play his *own* game only when he was sure that *everyone else* was playing their role as required, in the agreed-upon game plan and to the required performance level.

This contrasted vividly with the approach of a later captain, Gary Teichman, who himself seemed to play harder and better the worse his team performed. However laudable that was, he was out of synch, a pace too fast, a step out of position, or a fraction too early, for a successful continuation of play. It was heartbreaking to see such a gifted player dropped from the squad before the following World Cup because of his perceived inability to take everyone else with him. Gary's play was not inspiring enough on its own.

At its heart, captaincy involves devoting so much of your CEO time in making sure everyone is on the bus and in good voice. When everyone else has gone home, the lonely work of captaincy carries on in your own game, doing what you do best, in the knowledge that your launch pad is high, stable and well supported. It's closer to the stars and many more eyes will want to see you reach them, too.

89.

Non-executive directors

Having insiders or outsiders on the Board to fulfil the role of over-seers is one of the regulatory jokes played on business. No CEO wants a hostile Board. Those employed in the company are subservient in rank and dependent on his goodwill. He has less sway over those who get paid directors' emoluments, who can be removed or influenced, and have a great incentive to conform to the will of the Group for status and fees.

If the role of Non-Executive Directors (NEDs) is to gain the intended gravitas, several things need to happen.

Firstly, the NEDs should gain and demonstrate acute formal skills in assisting Board decisions. At the very least, this would probably mean acquiring updated and ongoing knowledge of the International Financial Reporting Standards (IFRS)international accounting standards, of legal issues pertaining to the enterprise and its industry, as well as great debating and decision-making skills and a track record of insight and guidance. In short, the NED must be a dedicated NED and not part of the furniture.

A deep and thorough understanding of the industry is required, which again shrinks the pool of talent that can be approached to serve on the Board.

Thirdly, there should be a time-limit on the tenure, or else objectivity could be compromised, the once sharp insights might become stale, be blunted, and the contributions diminish.

The probability is tiny of finding enough of these talented, in-profession, industry-savvy people. It is going to be troublesome finding such people in sufficient numbers, with capacity and inclination to support people they are unfamiliar with in a company they do not know intimately, and a management they do not yet trust.

The second-best choice, then, is an abdication to known and trusted people, who must make their own decisions on when to serve you loyally and when to serve shareholders. This is an easier choice for the CEO than for the NED, and it's inherently unfair but that's the way the system is set up. It is inexplicable and downright reckless that large shareholders, and especially institutional shareholders, have so often not developed and voted in their own representatives to serve their interests on Public Boards. The outcome is an unchecked escalation in and fees, to the detriment of shareholders and employees alike.

90.

DYNASTY

A special note for those owner-CEOs – an entrepreneurial species which I regard with the highest admiration. They are the backbone and future of any and every economy. Each of us has had a look at our progeny at some stage and wondered about two divergent choices, each of which comes with its own set of consequences and implications.

Should junior be led to on a path that will include furthering the corporation's future? One that will jump-start a possible dynasty?

Or else, should she be given the option of choosing her own future, knowing that Daddy and Mommy can afford to pay and help to lay the groundwork for it, and in all probability will do so?

I am faced with this very situation: with three blonde darlings and three hard choices. I have some ideas that could help, should you be set on building an empire to outlast you.

Decide early whether each youngster should follow the path to your throne. Leaving the vital talk until they turn 16 would be way too late. My friend Manny operates four large Spar supermarkets and his son has been accompanying Dad to open the stores since he turned two years old.

The first store is opened at 5 am. Young Pedro is now nine years old and is still doing the rounds before school. He works at one of the stores in the afternoon. He has no hobbies and plays no sport. The choices were made. The family is supportive and young Pedro is waxed for a career and an ambition to expand Dad's, and ultimately his, empire.

Imprint the special ideas you have on a budding mind. The normal and mundane interactions in business are beyond boring for a fertile mind. The extraordinary, the insightful and the wise things would be seeding an imagination that can, and will, embroider the fact that there is a head start in the making. The love of the enterprise often lies in the specialness of how it is steered and how things are done in special ways.

Prepare for a timeline that will suit all parties. Patriarch Anthony just brought David into his farming operations. David finished studying Rural Development in the UK and is returning to the non-metropolis of Viljoenskroon, farming population 3 000. His will be the fifth generation to run the farm. The business includes 5 000 hectares under cultivation, piggeries, factories and over 200 employees – a veritable empire. Anthony is 68; David 26. The overlap and the handover have been well planned. David will choose a South African wife – not a British girl, who would possibly find the transition to a small town community unfulfilling. Don't do the King Lear thing, either. It would be best if Dad found something else to do after the handover is complete.

Keep your expectations reasonable. We saw three generations of not-Henry Ford and countless examples of junior Big Shots – where offspring could never hope to take off and fly from the shoulders of self-made Billionaires. It may be hard to find the fine lines between spoiling and preparing, hunger and satisfaction, expectation and killer-pressure.

As a very, very late bloomer, I am thankful that my kids were born relatively late in my life. To have had a 16-year-old waiting for Dad's first breakthrough in hope of a later empire would have been stressful. Your goal should be to expect the best and prepare for the worst – to serve as a gentle and guiding light from their first day of school, until the keys are handed over in an elegant transition.

Along with her piano lessons, my eldest aims to type at 45 words per minute and lives for Lego Architecture between ballet and the pool. I guess she will enjoy the real estate development I have planned for her. The Second Born? Perhaps the mining supplies operation. The Third Born? Perhaps the telco business. Then again, I need to keep my expectations reasonable, even in a world with shrinking numbers of good jobs and a compliance culture that is demeaning and soul-destroying. We want the best for our children and it will help in preparing them for the real world if they can get to choose from some fantastic and exciting options.

In conclusion: lifestyle

CEOs aren't that different to cowboys. They know that they probably have only one chance at life. If everything works out, it could be a good one. A cowboy longs for a long, healthy and happy life. He knows that staying healthy and happy will contribute to a long life that was worth living. His happiness comes from the quiet satisfaction of a job well done and a life well lived. He'll call it contentment and indicate this with a modest smile and a shrug, and say he was just lucky all along; never mentioning that he knows deep down that luck comes from hard and persistent effort. He may be nonchalant over his health, but he exercises self-control and has a modest appetite. He knows himself, has made a career out of learning from his mistakes and moving on out of the past.

The cowboy is private with his ambitions. He's not looking for a break. He's creating his own. He knows that mastery of the skills that make up being a good cowboy will in time lead to the path of becoming a Great One. He doesn't fret about the slow, grinding and eventual sifting that life does to us all, in order to separate the best from the also-rans. He bides his time, honing his talents in the time-tested way, by using them. He knows the value and the importance of time, which waits for no man. He faithfully accounts for every minute. When the day is done, he contemplates it, filing away its lessons and reprimanding himself for those bad choices that led to mistakes he then had to fix.

He knows that a problem not solved will remain that way forever. That tackling the big problems, like all big ideas, may require the help of others. He shares some of his time setting a greenhorn straight, but never does what the other man can and should do for himself. He listens to and abides by the laws of nature. Shortcuts have their inherent risks. So, too, do long shots. Emergencies are where he draws on earned goodwill and ample, saved, resources. He is conservative in his ways and in the old sense: never wasting, never prying, leaving behind light footprints wherever he goes. His shadow falls on others and he may bestow good influence and fond memories without requiring a debt of reciprocity. Slow to speak and cautious with his opinions, he is humble in sharing them. He doesn't guess or speculate. He either knows the answer, or will find it.

Likewise, he is not easily swayed unless wisdom accompanies the facts. He defers his pleasures, denies himself the immediate enjoyment of the fruits of his labours, expecting his progeny to find his accumulated treasures of some use. He doesn't compete directly with others. He judges his actions only against his own standards. The cowboy lives by a set of principles and will not compromise these for gain. He is slow to take offence or make enemies, but quick to defend what is right, what is just and what is rightfully his, or under his protection. He thinks of himself last, and foolishly will risk all for his cause.

His solutions are simple and elegant and he relishes the tasks ahead. The cowboy knows that completion of a task is more valuable than just planning it, and that persistence is his greatest strength. He wastes no energy on the foolish or the seemingly impossible, unless the latter can be chunked down to the doable. His life is one of con-templated actions and he finds meaning and satisfaction in the jour-ney. He never breaks one thing to fix another. He understands the place and function of most things and would not operate something if he didn't understand it.

Perhaps he philosophises. More often, he just tries to understand the meaning and interconnectedness of the things that touch his life. He takes responsibility for everything he does and lives by the creed that every decision and action will have consequences, and may often have unforeseen ones, too. Therefore he plans ahead to minimise the risks, reducing the margin of error as he goes along by getting better, smarter and more efficient. Wisdom is understand-ing the **what** and the **why**. The former coming easily and the latter only yielding answers the way the earth gives up her bounty: slowly, reluctantly. It brings the fruits of the harvest which are priceless to possess.

Is he a force for good? He wouldn't say so himself, but others may do so and perhaps to his embarrassed face. He does what a man has to do, a special man, though he cannot think why all men don't see the easy logic of wanting such a life well-lived, with rewards earned. The ways of the charlatan and cheater baffle him. He is often unable to fathom their tricks and shuns them instead.

Death neither worries nor fascinates him. He sees, and often deals with it, on the range. The cycle of the grass is shorter than that of a man but is just as important. When feeling his youthful vigor slipping away, he accepts that a long life would be a curse without tasks to accomplish or the energy to do them. His life-long-learned expertise is easy to pass on to those he would welcome to stand on his shoulders, to reach for a better tomorrow in a better world than the one he found and changed.

This thought would be his last, as with a wry smile as he fades from this world and from the memory of those he touched. Home on his Range in the Sky, life below would keep on with its cycles, perhaps creating another like him, just better. That would be his final wish.

This is how I see the world. Maybe you do so too?

Good luck in everything you attempt. May you never run out of good plans.

Books that are timeless in their influence

Robert Townsend's **Up the Organization**. The 70's primer on common sense and how to run an organization like Avis. Indispensable, plain and devoid of nonsense. This was my inspiration to switch from studying Dentistry to Business – and I thank the Gods I did.

The Classic Touch: Lessons in Leadership by Clemens & Mayer. A finely honed set of lessons from those who shaped the known history

Bargaining for Results from that great master John Winkler. Everything you always wanted to know about the interaction of your value and your competitor's price.

Nassim Nicholas Taleb's seminal. *Antifragile*. The most important living philosopher takes on a horde of barbarian thoughts and tames them to servile needs. Breathless stuff explaining the real world.

Snorri Sturluson. *Haemskringla*. The 11th century sagas of the Norse kings that will dampen your woes in telling the stories of real issues that shaped kingdoms. It plumbs the depths of human connivance and fortitude.

In **Smile or Die** Barbara Ehrenreich explains the development of the work ethic, the rise of corporate happiness and the interchangeability of the CEO and the Church Minister in lucid detail.

*

Thank you for reading this book. Please share your thoughts and ideas with me? There are thousands of lessons out there and the experiences we share could move us to change our world for the better. I'm on Twitter: @unconCEO and my website is: www.MarioPretorius.co.za.